# The Ultimate CCNA Flash Cards Collection

Master Networking Essentials with Ease

1st Edition

www.ipspecialist.net

 

# Table of Contents



 

# Cisco Certifications

Cisco Systems, Inc. specializes in networking and communications products and services. A leader in global technology, the company is best known for its business routing and switching products that direct data, voice, and video traffic across networks worldwide.

Cisco also offers one of the world's most comprehensive vendor-specific certification programs, the *Cisco Career Certification program.* The program has six (6) levels, which begin at the Entry level and then advance to Associate, Professional, and Expert levels. For some certifications, the program closes at the Architect level.

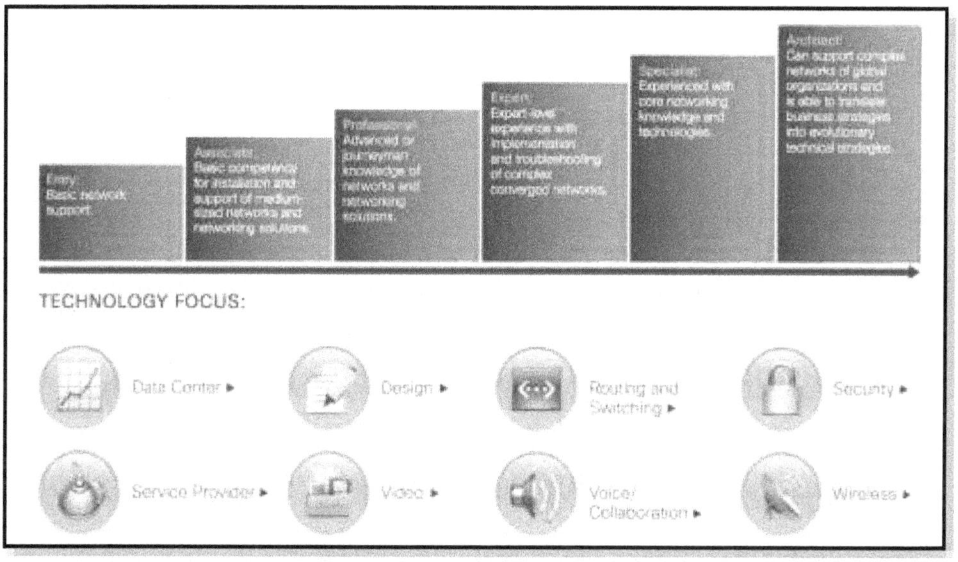


*Figure 1. Cisco Certifications Skill Matrix. Copyright 2013 by Cisco and/or its affiliates*

**How do Cisco certifications help?**

Cisco certifications are a de facto standard in the networking industry, which helps you boost your career in the following ways:

1. Gets your foot in the door by launching your IT career
2. Boosts your confidence level
3. Proves knowledge that helps improve employment opportunities

As for companies, Cisco certification is a way to:

1. Screen job applicants
2. Validate the technical skills of the candidate

 

3. Ensure quality, competency, and relevancy
4. Improve organization credibility and customers loyalty
5. Meet the requirement in maintaining organization partnership level with OEMs
6. Helps in Job retention and promotion

**Cisco Certification Tracks**

| Certification Tracks | Entry | Associate | Professional | Expert | Architect |
|---|---|---|---|---|---|
| Collaboration | | | | CCIE Collaboration | |
| Data Center | | CCNA Data Center | CCNP Data Center | CCIE Data Center | |
| Design | CCENT | CCDA | CCDP | CCDE | CCAr |
| Routing & Switching | CCENT | CCNA Routing and Switching | CCNP | CCIE Routing & Switching | |
| Security | CCENT | CCNA Security | CCNP Security | CCIE Security | |
| Service Provider | | CCNA Service Provider | CCNP Service Provider | CCIE Service Provider | |
| Service Provider Operations | CCENT | CCNA Service Provider Operations | CCNP Service Provider Operations | CCIE Service Provider Operations | |
| Video | | CCNA Video | | | |
| Voice | CCENT | CCNA Voice | CCNP Voice | CCIE Voice | |
| Wireless | CCENT | CCNA Wireless | CCNP Wireless | CCIE Wireless | |

*Figure 2. Cisco Certifications Track*

## How to become a CCNA?

### Step 1: Pre-requisites

No prior certification is required, although it is advised to have at least a year's worth of Cisco solution administration and implementation expertise.

### Step 2: Prepare for the CCNP SPRI Exam

Exam preparation can be accomplished through self-study with textbooks, practice exams, and on-site classroom programs. This workbook provides you with all the information and knowledge to help you pass the CCNA Exam. Your study will be divided into two distinct parts:

- Understanding the technologies as per the exam blueprint
- Implementing and practicing the technologies on Network Simulator (EVE-NG)

 

IPSpecialist provides full support to the candidates in order for them to pass the exam.

**Step 3: Register for the exam**

Certification exams are offered at locations throughout the world. To register for an exam, contact the authorized test delivery partner of Cisco contact *Pearson VUE*, who will administer the exam in a secure, proctored environment.

Prior to registration, decide which exam to take, and note the exam name and number. For complete exam details, refer to the "Current Exam List" from the Cisco website.

Other important details to note are the following:

1. Your personal information prior to the exam registration
    a. Legal name (from government issued ID)
    b. Cisco Certification ID (i.e., CSCO00000001) or Test ID number
    c. Company name
    d. Valid email address
    e. Method of payment
2. To prevent duplicate records and delays in receiving proper credit for your exams, please locate your Cisco Certification ID (for example, CSCO00000001) before proceeding with your registration if you have already completed a Cisco exam.
3. When registering for the exam, a working email is essential. When a candidate's certification is set to expire, Cisco needs to know this to send email reminders, confirm the mailing address before sending the certificate, and notify candidates if their certificate was returned due to an inaccurate address.
4. Pearson VUE is the authorized test delivery partner of Cisco. You may register online, by telephone, or by walk-in (where available).

***How much does an exam cost?***

Computer-based certification exam prices (written exam) depend on scope and exam length. You may refer to the "Exam Pricing" page on the Cisco website for complete details.

**Step 4: Getting the Results**

After you complete an exam at an authorized testing centre, you will get immediate online notification of your pass or fail status, a printed examination

 

score report that indicates your pass or fail status, and your exam results by section.
Congratulations!!! You are CCNA Certified.

## About Cisco Certified: CCNA: Cisco Certified Network Associate (Exam: 200-301)

| | |
|---|---|
| **Exam Questions** | Case study, short answer, repeated answer, MCQs |
| **Number of Questions** | 100 |
| **Time to Complete** | 120 minutes |
| **Exam Fee** | 300 USD + tax |

The CCNA Exam v1.0 (CCNA 200-301) is a 120-minute exam related to the CCNA certification. This exam assesses a candidate's knowledge and abilities in relation to network accessibility, IP connection, IP services, security basics, automation, and programmability. The Implementing and Administering Cisco Solutions (CCNA) course aids applicants in getting ready for this exam.
The broad guidelines below outline the subject that is most likely to be covered on the exam. On any particular exam delivery, though, additional relevant topics might potentially show up. The guidelines below may change without prior notice to reflect the exam's subject matter more accurately and for clarity.

- Network Fundamentals (20%)
- Network Access (20%)
- IP Connectivity (25%)
- IP Services (10%)
- Security Fundamentals (15%)
- Automation and Programmability (10%)

## Recommended Knowledge

- Explain the role and function of network components
- Describe characteristics of network topology architectures
- Compare physical interface and cabling types

 

- Identify interface and cable issues (collisions, errors, mismatch duplex, and/or speed)
- Compare TCP to UDP
- Configure and verify IPv4 addressing and subnetting
- Describe the need for private IPv4 addressing
- Configure and verify IPv6 addressing and prefix
- Describe IPv6 address types
- Verify IP parameters for Client OS (Windows, Mac OS, Linux)
- Describe wireless principles
- Explain virtualization fundamentals (server virtualization, containers, and VRFs)
- Describe switching concepts
- Configure and verify VLANs (normal range) spanning multiple switches
- Configure and verify interswitch connectivity
- Configure and verify Layer 2 discovery protocols (Cisco Discovery Protocol and LLDP)
- Configure and verify (Layer 2/Layer 3) EtherChannel (LACP)
- Interpret basic operations of Rapid PVST+ Spanning Tree Protocol
- Describe Cisco Wireless Architectures and AP modes
- Describe physical infrastructure connections of WLAN components (AP, WLC, access/trunk ports, and LAG)
- Describe AP and WLC management access connections (Telnet, SSH, HTTP, HTTPS, console, and TACACS+/RADIUS)
- Interpret the wireless LAN GUI configuration for client connectivity, such as WLAN creation, security settings, QoS profiles, and advanced settings
- Interpret the components of routing table
- Determine how a router makes a forwarding decision by default
- Configure and verify IPv4 and IPv6 static routing
- Configure and verify single area OSPFv2
- Describe the purpose, functions, and concepts of first hop redundancy protocols
- Configure and verify inside source NAT using static and pools
- Configure and verify NTP operating in a client and server mode
- Explain the role of DHCP and DNS within the network
- Explain the function of SNMP in network operations

 

- Describe the use of syslog features including facilities and levels
- Configure and verify DHCP client and relay
- Explain the forwarding per-hop behavior (PHB) for QoS, such as classification, marking, queuing, congestion, policing, and shaping
- Configure network devices for remote access using SSH
- Describe the capabilities and functions of TFTP/FTP in the network
- Define key security concepts (threats, vulnerabilities, exploits, and mitigation techniques)
- Describe security program elements (user awareness, training, and physical access control)
- Configure and verify device access control using local passwords
- Describe security password policies elements, such as management, complexity, and password alternatives (multifactor authentication, certificates, and biometrics)
- Describe IPsec remote access and site-to-site VPNs
- Configure and verify access control lists
- Configure and verify Layer 2 security features (DHCP snooping, dynamic ARP inspection, and port security)
- Compare authentication, authorization, and accounting concepts
- Describe wireless security protocols (WPA, WPA2, and WPA3)
- Configure and verify WLAN within the GUI using WPA2 PSK
- Explain how automation impacts network management
- Compare traditional networks with controller-based networking
- Describe controller-based, software defined architecture (overlay, underlay, and fabric)
- Compare traditional campus device management with Cisco DNA Center enabled device management
- Describe characteristics of REST-based APIs (CRUD, HTTP verbs, and data encoding)
- Recognize the capabilities of configuration management mechanisms Puppet, Chef, and Ansible
- Recognize components of JSON-encoded data

 

All the required information is included in this Study Guide.

| | Domain | Percentage |
|---|---|---|
| **Domain 1** | Network Fundamentals | 20% |
| **Domain 2** | Network Access | 20% |
| **Domain 3** | IP Connectivity | 25% |
| **Domain 4** | IP Services | 10% |
| **Domain 5** | Security Fundamentals | 15% |
| **Domain 6** | Automation and Programmability | 10% |

 

# Section – 1: Network Fundamentals

 

**Flash Card # 1**
**Term:** Network Interface Card (NIC)
**Function:** Connects a device to a network, providing physical layer and data link layer functionalities.

**Flash Card # 2**
**Term:** Switch
**Function:** Learns MAC addresses of connected devices and forwards data packets to specific ports based on their destination addresses (Layer 2 device).

**Flash Card # 3**
**Term:** Router
**Function:** Connects different networks and forwards data packets based on their IP addresses (Layer 3 device).

**Flash Card # 4**
**Term:** Network Interface Card (NIC)
**Function:** Connects a device to a network, providing physical layer and data link layer functionalities.

**Flash Card #5**
**Term:** Switch

 

**Function:** Learns MAC addresses of connected devices and forwards data packets to specific ports based on their destination addresses (Layer 2 device).

**Flash Card #6**

**Term:** Router

**Function:** Connects different networks and forwards data packets based on their IP addresses (Layer 3 device).

**Flash Card #7**

**Term:** Hub

**Function:** Simple device that broadcasts all data packets received on one port to all other ports (mostly outdated technology).

**Flash Card #8**

**Term:** Firewall

**Function:** Monitors incoming and outgoing network traffic, enforcing security policies to block unwanted traffic.

**Flash Card #9**

**Term:** Access Point (AP)

**Function:** Creates a wireless local area network (WLAN) by providing Wi-Fi connectivity to devices.

 

**Flash Card #10**

**Term:** Modem

**Function:** Modulates and demodulates signals, allowing data transmission over different mediums like cable or phone lines.

**Flash Card #11**

**Term:** Server

**Function:** Provides resources or services to other devices on the network, like file sharing, email, or web hosting.

**Flash Card #12**

**Term:** Client

**Function:** Requests resources or services from servers on the network (e.g., your laptop accessing a printer).

**Flash Card #13**

**Term:** Cable

**Function:** Physical medium used to connect network devices together, like Ethernet cables or fiber optic cables.

**Flash Card #14**

**Term:** Domain Name System (DNS)

 

**Function:** Translates human-readable domain names (like [invalid URL removed]) into machine-readable IP addresses.

**Flash Card #15**
**Term:** Dynamic Host Configuration Protocol (DHCP)
**Function:** Automatically assigns IP addresses and other configuration settings to devices on a network.

**Flash Card #16**
**Term:** Network Address Translation (NAT)
**Function:** Allows multiple devices on a private network to share a single public IP address for internet access.

**Flash Card #17**
**Term:** Load Balancer
**Function:** Distributes incoming network traffic across multiple servers to optimize performance and prevent overload.

**Flash Card #18**
**Term:** VPN (Virtual Private Network)
**Function:** Creates a secure encrypted tunnel over the internet, allowing remote users to connect to a private network.

 

### Flash Card #19

**Term:** Repeater

**Function:** Extends the range of a wireless signal by amplifying and retransmitting it.

### Flash Card #20

**Term:** Gateway

**Function:** Acts as a passage between different networks, often used interchangeably with router but can also refer to a device connecting a network to the internet.

### Flash Card #21

**Term:** Firewall Appliance

**Function:** A dedicated hardware device specifically designed for network security and firewall functionalities.

### Flash Card #22

**Term:** Intrusion Detection System (IDS)

**Function:** Monitors network traffic for suspicious activity and potential security threats.

### Flash Card #23

**Term:** Intrusion Prevention System (IPS)

 

**Function:** Not only detects but also actively prevents security threats by blocking malicious traffic.

**Flash Card #24**
**Term:** VLAN (Virtual Local Area Network)
**Function:** Logically segments a network into smaller broadcast domains, improving security and network performance.

**Flash Card #25**
**Term:** Spanning Tree Protocol (STP)
**Function:** Prevents loops in switched networks by ensuring there's only one active path for data flow.

**Flash Card #26**
**Term:** Protocol
**Function:** A set of rules and procedures that govern how devices communicate and exchange data on a network.

**Flash Card #27**
**Term:** Network Management System (NMS)
**Function:** Provides centralized monitoring and management of network devices and resources.

 

### Flash Card #28

**Term:** Content Delivery Network (CDN)
**Function:** Geographically distributed network of servers that stores cached content to deliver webpages and other online resources faster to users.

### Flash Card #29

**Term:** Network Attached Storage (NAS)
**Function:** Dedicated file-level storage device attached to a network, providing shared storage for users and applications.

### Flash Card #30

**Term:** Session Initiation Protocol (SIP)
**Function:** Enables and manages voice and video communication sessions over IP networks (like VoIP calls).

### Flash Card #31

**Term:** Border Gateway Protocol (BGP)
**Function:** Routing protocol used between autonomous systems (AS) on the internet to exchange routing information and determine the best path for data delivery.

### Flash Card #32

**Term:** Quality of Service (QoS)

 

**Function:** Techniques to prioritize and manage network traffic to ensure consistent performance for critical applications like voice and video conferencing.

**Flash Card #33**

**Term:** High Availability (HA)

**Function:** Design principle that ensures continuous operation of critical systems and applications by minimizing downtime in case of failures.

**Flash Card #34**

**Term:** Software-Defined Networking (SDN)

**Function:** Network architecture that separates the control plane (network intelligence) from the data plane (data forwarding) allowing for more programmable and flexible networks.

**Flash Card #35**

**Term:** Network Function Virtualization (NFV)

**Function:** Virtualizes network functions like firewalls and load balancers, allowing them to run on standard servers instead of dedicated hardware.

**Flash Card #36**

**Term:** Application Delivery Controller (ADC)

**Function:** Optimizes the delivery of applications by balancing traffic across servers, providing security features, and offloading processing tasks.

 

## Flash Card #37

**Term:** Wireless Local Area Network (WLAN)

**Function:** Network that uses radio waves instead of cables to provide wireless connectivity to devices within a limited area.

## Flash Card #38

**Term:** Encryption

**Function:** Scrambles data using algorithms and keys, making it unreadable to unauthorized users.

## Flash Card #39

**Term:** Decryption

**Function:** Process of transforming encrypted data back to its original form using the corresponding decryption key.

## Flash Card #40

**Term:** Authentication

**Function:** Verifies the identity of a user or device attempting to access a network or resource.

## Flash Card #41

**Term:** Authorization

**Function:** Determines the level of access granted to a user or device once their identity is verified.

 

### Flash Card #42

**Term:** Access Control List (ACL)

**Function:** Set of rules that define which network traffic is allowed or denied on a network device.

### Flash Card #43

**Term:** Demilitarized Zone (DMZ)

**Function:** Subnet that sits between a public network and a private network, isolating critical internal resources from external threats.

### Flash Card #44

**Term:** Denial-of-Service (DoS) Attack

**Function:** Attempt to overwhelm a network or server with traffic, making it unavailable to legitimate users.

### Flash Card #45

**Term:** Man-in-the-Middle (MitM) Attack

**Function:** Eavesdropping attack where an attacker intercepts communication between two parties and potentially alters the data.

 

**Flash Card #46**
**Term:** Phishing Attack
**Function:** Deceptive email or message designed to trick users into revealing sensitive information like passwords or credit card details.

**Flash Card #47**
**Term:** Social Engineering
**Function:** Psychological manipulation techniques used to trick users into granting access or divulging confidential information.

**Flash Card #48**
**Term:** Bandwidth
**Function:** Measured in bits per second (bps), it signifies the maximum data transfer rate possible on a network connection.

**Flash Card #49**
**Term:** Latency
**Function:** Refers to the time delay it takes for data to travel from one point to another on a network, measured in milliseconds (ms).

**Flash Card #50**
**Term:** Throughput

 

**Function:** Represents the actual amount of data successfully transmitted over a network connection within a given time, typically measured in Mbps (megabits per second).

## Flash Card #51

**Term:** Packet Loss

**Function:** Occurs when data packets travelling across the network fail to reach their destination.

## Flash Card #52

**Term:** Jitter

**Function:** Variation in the time it takes for data packets to travel across the network, causing inconsistencies in data flow and impacting performance.

## Flash Card #53

**Term:** Ping

**Function:** A diagnostic tool used to test connectivity between two network devices by sending and receiving data packets.

## Flash Card #54

**Term:** Traceroute

**Function:** Utility that reveals the path a data packet takes to reach its destination, helping identify network route issues.

 

## Flash Card #55

**Term:** Network Monitoring Tools

**Function:** Software applications used to monitor network performance, identify potential problems, and ensure network health.

## Flash Card #56

**Term:** Cable Tester

**Function:** Electronic device used to diagnose physical problems with network cables, ensuring proper signal transmission.

## Flash Card #57

**Term:** Event Logs

**Function:** Records of network activity and events generated by network devices, providing valuable information for troubleshooting purposes.

## Flash Card #58

**Term:** Multiprotocol Label Switching (MPLS)

**Function:** Advanced routing technique that utilizes labels for faster and more efficient data forwarding across networks.

 

### Flash Card #59

**Term:** Software-Defined Wide Area Network (SD-WAN)
**Function:** Network architecture that applies SDN principles to WANs, allowing for dynamic and centralized control of geographically dispersed networks.

### Flash Card #60

**Term:** Network Segmentation
**Function:** Dividing a network into smaller subnets to improve security, performance, and manageability.

### Flash Card #61

**Term:** Network Address Translation (NAT) Types

- **Static NAT:** Assigns fixed public IP addresses to specific devices on a private network.
- **Dynamic NAT:** Assigns public IP addresses from a pool to devices on a private network on a temporary basis.
- **Port Address Translation (PAT):** Maps multiple private IP addresses and ports to a single public IP address for internet access.

### Flash Card #62

**Term:** Virtualization Technologies

- **Network virtualization:** Creates virtual networks on top of a physical network infrastructure.
- **Server virtualization:** Allows running multiple virtual servers on a single physical server.

 

## Flash Card #63

**Term:** Internet of Things (IoT)

**Function:** Network of physical devices embedded with sensors and software, enabling them to collect and exchange data.

## Flash Card #64

**Term:** Network Function Virtualization (NFV) Orchestration

**Function:** Automated management and provisioning of virtualized network functions (VNFs) on an NFV infrastructure.

## Flash Card #65

**Term:** Cloud Security

**Function:** Practices and technologies to protect data, applications, and resources stored or accessed in the cloud.

## Flash Card #66

**Term:** Network Automation

**Function:** Utilizing scripting languages and tools to automate network configuration, management, and troubleshooting tasks.

## Flash Card #67

**Term:** Infrastructure as Code (IaC)

**Function:** Managing network infrastructure through code, enabling consistent and automated deployments.

 

**Flash Card #68**

**Term:** IEEE 802.11 Standards

**Function:** A family of Wi-Fi standards defining different wireless networking technologies like 802.11a/b/g/n/ac for varying speeds and frequencies.

**Flash Card #69**

**Term:** Service Set Identifier (SSID)

**Function:** Unique identifier that identifies a specific wireless network.

**Flash Card #70**

**Term:** Access Point (AP) Modes

- **Access Point (Managed Mode):** Traditional mode where the AP creates a wireless network for clients to connect.
- **Wireless Repeater Mode:** Extends the range of an existing wireless network by amplifying and retransmitting the signal.
- **Wireless Bridge Mode:** Connects two wired networks wirelessly, often used to extend wired connectivity.

**Flash Card #71**

**Term:** Wireless Security Protocols

- **WEP (Wired Equivalent Privacy):** An outdated and easily compromised security protocol.
- **WPA (Wi-Fi Protected Access):** More secure than WEP, offering encryption and authentication mechanisms.
- **WPA2 (Wi-Fi Protected Access 2):** Enhanced version of WPA with stronger encryption using AES algorithms.

 

## Flash Card #72

**Term:** Mesh Networking

**Function:** A network topology where devices connect with each other wirelessly, creating a decentralized and self-healing network.

## Flash Card #73

**Router:**

- **Role:** Routes data between different networks.
- **Function:** Determines the best path for data packets to reach their destination based on network addresses.

## Flash Card #74

**Switch:**

- **Role:** Connects devices within the same network.
- **Function:** Forwards data packets to the appropriate device based on MAC addresses.

## Flash Card #75

**Hub:**

- **Role:** Connects multiple devices in a network.
- **Function:** Broadcasts data packets to all connected devices, regardless of the destination.

## Flash Card #76

**Firewall:**

- **Role:** Protects the network from unauthorized access and external threats.
- **Function:** Filters incoming and outgoing traffic based on predefined security rules.

## Flash Card #77

**Modem:**

- **Role:** Converts digital data from a computer into analog signals for transmission over telephone lines (for DSL) or cable lines (for cable internet).
- **Function:** Modulates and demodulates signals to facilitate communication between devices over a network.\

## Flash Card #78

**Access Point:**

- **Role:** Provides wireless connectivity to devices within a network.
- **Function:** Transmits and receives data between wireless devices and the wired network infrastructure.

## Flash Card #79

**Network Interface Card (NIC):**

- **Role:** Connects a device to a network.

 

- **Function:** Translates data between the device's internal communication system and the network.

## Flash Card #80

**Gateway:**

- **Role:** Connects different types of networks.
- **Function:** Acts as an entry and exit point for data traffic between networks with different protocols or architectures.

## Flash Card #81

**Load Balancer:**

- **Role:** Distributes incoming network traffic across multiple servers or resources to optimize performance and reliability.
- **Function:** Monitors server health and usage and directs traffic to the most available and least busy servers.

## Flash Card #82

**Patch Panel:**

- **Role:** Provides a centralized location for connecting and managing network cables.
- **Function:** Allows network administrators to easily route and reconfigure network connections without physically moving devices.

 

### Flash Card #83

**Repeater:**

- **Role:** Regenerates and amplifies signals to extend the reach of a network.
- **Function:** Receives weak signals, amplifies them, and retransmits them to maintain signal strength over long distances.

### Flash Card #84

**Proxy Server:**

- **Role:** Acts as an intermediary between client devices and the internet.
- **Function:** Caches frequently accessed web content, filters incoming and outgoing traffic, and enhances security and privacy by masking client IP addresses.

### Flash Card#85

**Network Attached Storage (NAS):**

- **Role:** Provides centralized storage accessible over a network.
- **Function:** Stores and retrieves data from multiple devices on the network, serving as a shared storage resource for users and applications.

### Flash Card #86

**Content Delivery Network (CDN):**

- **Role:** Improves the delivery speed and reliability of web content.

 

- **Function:** Stores cached copies of web content on servers distributed across multiple locations, reducing latency and bandwidth usage for end users.

## Flash Card #87

**Load Balancer:**

- **Role:** Distributes incoming network traffic across multiple servers or resources to optimize performance and reliability.
- **Function:** Monitors server health and usage and directs traffic to the most available and least busy servers.

## Flash Card #88

**Virtual Private Network (VPN):**

- **Role:** Creates a secure, encrypted connection over a public network, such as the internet.
- **Function:** Provides remote users with secure access to a private network, enabling secure communication and data transfer over untrusted networks.

## Flash Card #89

**Domain Name System (DNS) Server:**

- **Role:** Translates domain names into IP addresses.
- **Function:** Resolves domain names to their corresponding IP addresses, allowing users to access websites and other resources using human-readable names.

 

## Flash Card #90

**Network Time Protocol (NTP) Server:**

- **Role:** Synchronizes the time across devices on a network.
- **Function:** Provides accurate timekeeping by distributing time signals from a reliable time source to network devices, ensuring synchronization and consistency.

## Flash Card #91

**Intrusion Detection System (IDS):**

- **Role:** Monitors network traffic for suspicious activity and potential security threats.
- **Function:** Analyzes network packets and events to detect and alert administrators to unauthorized access attempts, malware infections, and other security breaches.

## Flash Card #92

**Intrusion Prevention System (IPS):**

- **Role:** Prevents malicious activity and security breaches on a network.
- **Function:** Monitors and filters network traffic in real-time, blocking or mitigating security threats such as denial-of-service attacks, malware infections, and unauthorized access attempts.

 

## Flash Card #93

**Ethernet Cable:**

- **Role:** Connects devices within a network.
- **Function:** Transmits data packets between devices using electrical signals over twisted pairs of copper wires.

## Flash Card #94

**Fiber Optic Cable:**

- **Role:** Transmits data over long distances with high speed and bandwidth.
- **Function:** Uses light signals to transmit data through thin strands of glass or plastic fibers, offering immunity to electromagnetic interference and enabling faster data transmission rates.

## Flash Card #95

**Managed Switch:**

- **Role:** Provides advanced network management features and capabilities.
- **Function:** Allows network administrators to configure VLANs, implement Quality of Service (QoS), and monitor and manage network traffic more granularly compared to unmanaged switches.

 

## Flash Card #96

**Uninterruptible Power Supply (UPS):**

- **Role:** Provides backup power in case of electrical outages or fluctuations.
- **Function:** Supplies continuous power to network devices, such as routers, switches, and servers, ensuring uninterrupted operation and protecting against data loss or downtime during power interruptions.

## Flash Card #97

**Wireless Router:**

- **Role:** Connects devices wirelessly to a network.
- **Function:** Acts as a central hub for wireless communication, allowing devices such as laptops, smartphones, and tablets to connect to the internet and communicate with each other over Wi-Fi.

## Flash Card #98

**Network Attached Storage (NAS):**

- **Role:** Provides centralized storage accessible over a network.
- **Function:** Stores and retrieves data from multiple devices on the network, serving as a shared storage resource for users and applications.

 

## Flash Card #99

**Print Server:**

- **Role:** Manages printing tasks and resources on a network.
- **Function:** Stores and manages print jobs, provides print queues, and controls access to network printers, allowing multiple users to share printing resources efficiently.

## Flash Card #100

**Packet Sniffer:**

- **Role:** Captures and analyzes network traffic for troubleshooting, security, and performance monitoring purposes.
- **Function:** Intercepts and inspects data packets flowing through a network, providing insights into network behavior, identifying anomalies, and diagnosing issues such as network congestion or security breaches.

## Flash Card #101

**Terminal Server:**

- **Role:** Allows remote access to network resources and applications.
- **Function:** Provides a centralized platform for users to connect to network servers and applications remotely, facilitating remote administration, troubleshooting, and access to centralized resources.

 

## Flash Card #102

**VoIP Gateway:**

- **Role:** Converts analog voice signals into digital data packets for transmission over IP networks.
- **Function:** Bridges traditional telephony networks with Voice over IP (VoIP) networks, enabling voice communication over the internet and facilitating the integration of voice and data services.

## Flash Card #103

**Proxy Server:**

- **Role:** Acts as an intermediary between client devices and the internet.
- **Function:** Caches frequently accessed web content, filters incoming and outgoing traffic, and enhances security and privacy by masking client IP addresses.

## Flash Card # 104

**Content Delivery Network (CDN):**

- **Role:** Improves the delivery speed and reliability of web content.
- **Function:** Stores cached copies of web content on servers distributed across multiple locations, reducing latency and bandwidth usage for end users.

 

## Flash Card # 105

**Load Balancer:**

- **Role:** Distributes incoming network traffic across multiple servers or resources to optimize performance and reliability.
- **Function:** Monitors server health and usage and directs traffic to the most available and least busy servers.

## Flash Card # 106

**Virtual Private Network (VPN):**

- **Role:** Creates a secure, encrypted connection over a public network, such as the internet.
- **Function:** Provides remote users with secure access to a private network, enabling secure communication and data transfer over untrusted networks.

## Flash Card # 107

**Domain Name System (DNS) Server:**

- **Role:** Translates domain names into IP addresses.
- **Function:** Resolves domain names to their corresponding IP addresses, allowing users to access websites and other resources using human-readable names.

## Flash Card # 108

**Network Time Protocol (NTP) Server:**

- **Role:** Synchronizes the time across devices on a network.

 

- **Function:** Provides accurate timekeeping by distributing time signals from a reliable time source to network devices, ensuring synchronization and consistency.

**Flash Card # 109**

**Intrusion Detection System (IDS):**

- **Role:** Monitors network traffic for suspicious activity and potential security threats.
- **Function:** Analyzes network packets and events to detect and alert administrators to unauthorized access attempts, malware infections, and other security breaches.

**Flash Card # 110**

**Intrusion Prevention System (IPS):**

- **Role:** Prevents malicious activity and security breaches on a network.
- **Function:** Monitors and filters network traffic in real-time, blocking or mitigating security threats such as denial-of-service attacks, malware infections, and unauthorized access attempts.

**Flash Card # 111**

**Patch Panel:**

- **Role:** Provides a centralized location for connecting and managing network cables.
- **Function:** Allows network administrators to easily route and reconfigure network connections without physically moving devices.

 

### Flash Card # 112

**Wireless Access Point Controller:**

- **Role:** Manages multiple wireless access points (APs) in a wireless network.
- **Function:** Centralizes configuration, monitoring, and management of APs, enabling seamless roaming, load balancing, and security enforcement in large-scale wireless deployments.

### Flash Card # 113

**Network Attached Storage (NAS):**

- **Role:** Provides centralized storage accessible over a network.
- **Function:** Stores and retrieves data from multiple devices on the network, serving as a shared storage resource for users and applications.

### Flash Card # 114

**Print Server:**

- **Role:** Manages printing tasks and resources on a network.
- **Function:** Stores and manages print jobs, provides print queues, and controls access to network printers, allowing multiple users to share printing resources efficiently.

### Flash Card # 115

**Packet Sniffer:**

- **Role:** Captures and analyzes network traffic for troubleshooting, security, and performance monitoring purposes.

 

- **Function:** Intercepts and inspects data packets flowing through a network, providing insights into network behavior, identifying anomalies, and diagnosing issues such as network congestion or security breaches.

## Flash Card # 116

**Terminal Server:**

- **Role:** Allows remote access to network resources and applications.
- **Function:** Provides a centralized platform for users to connect to network servers and applications remotely, facilitating remote administration, troubleshooting, and access to centralized resources.

## Flash Card # 117

**VoIP Gateway:**

- **Role:** Converts analog voice signals into digital data packets for transmission over IP networks.
- **Function:** Bridges traditional telephony networks with Voice over IP (VoIP) networks, enabling voice communication over the internet and facilitating the integration of voice and data services.

## Flash Card # 118

**Multiplexer (MUX):**

- **Role:** Combines multiple data streams into a single signal for transmission over a shared medium.
- **Function:** Allows efficient use of bandwidth by transmitting multiple signals simultaneously over a single communication channel, reducing costs and simplifying network infrastructure.

 

### Flash Card # 119

**Demultiplexer (DEMUX):**

- **Role:** Separates a single multiplexed signal into multiple data streams.
- **Function:** Extracts individual data streams from a multiplexed signal, allowing recipients to receive and process their intended data packets.

### Flash Card # 120

**Ethernet Switch (Layer 2 Switch):**

- **Role:** Connects devices within a local area network (LAN).
- **Function:** Forwards data packets between devices based on their MAC addresses, enabling efficient and secure communication within the network.

### Flash Card # 121

**Layer 3 Switch (Routing Switch):**

- **Role:** Combines the functions of a switch and a router.
- **Function:** Routes data packets between different networks based on their IP addresses, allowing for inter-network communication and traffic management.

### Flash Card # 122

**Power over Ethernet (PoE) Injector:**

- **Role:** Provides power to network devices over Ethernet cables.
- **Function:** Eliminates the need for separate power cables by delivering electrical power along with data signals, simplifying

 

installation and reducing costs for PoE-compatible devices such as IP cameras, VoIP phones, and wireless access points.

## Flash Card # 123

**Bus Topology:**

- **Characteristic:** Uses a single cable as a backbone to connect all devices in a linear manner.
- **Advantage:** Simple to implement and cost-effective for small networks.
- **Disadvantage:** Susceptible to cable failures, limited scalability, and performance degradation with increased network traffic.

## Flash Card # 124

**Star Topology:**

- **Characteristic:** Connects all devices to a central hub or switch.
- **Advantage:** Easy to troubleshoot, scalable, and allows for centralized management.
- **Disadvantage:** Relies heavily on the central hub, which can become a single point of failure.

## Flash Card # 125

**Ring Topology:**

- **Characteristic:** Connects devices in a circular configuration, where each device is connected to exactly two neighboring devices.
- **Advantage:** Equal access to network resources, efficient data transmission without collisions.

 

- **Disadvantage:** Vulnerable to cable failures, difficult to troubleshoot, and limited scalability.

**Flash Card # 126**

**Mesh Topology:**

- **Characteristic:** Connects every device to every other device in a fully interconnected network.
- **Advantage:** Redundant paths ensure high reliability and fault tolerance.
- **Disadvantage:** Complex to design and implement, requires a large number of cables and ports.

**Flash Card # 127**

**Hybrid Topology:**

- **Characteristic:** Combines two or more different topology types into a single network.
- **Advantage:** Offers flexibility to meet specific network requirements and optimize performance.
- **Disadvantage:** Can be more complex to manage and troubleshoot due to the combination of different topologies.

**Flash Card # 128**

**Mesh Topology (Partial):**

- **Characteristic:** Connects some devices to every other device in a partially interconnected network.
- **Advantage:** Provides redundancy and fault tolerance while reducing the complexity of a full mesh.

 

- **Disadvantage:** Less redundancy compared to a full mesh, may still require substantial cabling.

**Flash Card # 129**

**Tree Topology:**

- **Characteristic:** Organizes devices in a hierarchical structure, resembling a tree with branches and leaves.
- **Advantage:** Scalable and efficient for large networks, with clear hierarchies for management.
    - **Disadvantage:** Dependency on the root node, which can lead to network disruptions if it fails.

**Flash Card # 130**

**Point-to-Point Topology:**

- **Characteristic:** Connects two devices directly with a dedicated link.
- **Advantage:** Simple and straightforward, ideal for connecting remote locations over long distances.
- **Disadvantage:** Limited scalability, as each connection requires a dedicated link.

**Flash Card # 131**

**Fully Connected Topology:**

- **Characteristic:** Connects every device to every other device in the network.
- **Advantage:** Provides the highest level of redundancy and fault tolerance.

 

- **Disadvantage:** Requires a large number of connections, making it expensive and difficult to scale.

## Flash Card # 132

**Star-Ring Topology:**

- **Characteristic:** Combines the star and ring topologies, where devices are connected to a central hub in a star configuration and the hubs are interconnected in a ring.
- **Advantage:** Provides redundancy and fault tolerance while maintaining centralized management.
- **Disadvantage:** Complexity increases with the addition of ring interconnections.

## Flash Card # 133

**Dual Ring Topology:**

- **Characteristic:** Consists of two interconnected rings, providing redundancy and fault tolerance.
- **Advantage:** Offers continuous network operation even if one ring fails.
- **Disadvantage:** Requires additional hardware and complexity compared to a single ring.

## Flash Card # 134

**Hierarchical Topology:**

- **Characteristic:** Organizes devices into multiple layers or levels, with each layer serving a specific function.

 

- **Advantage:** Facilitates scalable network design, improves performance, and simplifies management.
- **Disadvantage:** Complexity increases with the number of layers, and changes to the hierarchy may require significant reconfiguration.

## Flash Card # 135

**Mesh Underlay Topology:**

- **Characteristic:** Provides a foundation for overlay networks by establishing connectivity between network nodes.
- **Advantage:** Supports dynamic routing and efficient traffic distribution in overlay networks.
- **Disadvantage:** Complexity increases with the number of nodes and connections.

## Flash Card # 136

**Cluster Topology:**

- **Characteristic:** Groups devices into clusters or nodes, where each cluster communicates with other clusters through designated gateway nodes.
- **Advantage:** Enhances scalability, fault tolerance, and load balancing.
- **Disadvantage:** Requires careful planning and configuration to ensure proper cluster communication and management.

 

## Flash Card # 137

**Star-Bus Topology:**

- **Characteristic:** Combines the star and bus topologies, with devices connected to a central hub in a star configuration and the hub connected to a shared bus.
- **Advantage:** Provides redundancy and fault tolerance while allowing for easy expansion and scalability.
- **Disadvantage:** Susceptible to cable failures on the shared bus segment.

## Flash Card # 138

**Daisy Chain Topology:**

- **Characteristic:** Connects devices in a linear fashion, with each device connected to the next in a chain.
- **Advantage:** Simple and easy to set up, suitable for small networks with few devices.
- **Disadvantage:** Vulnerable to cable failures, and network performance may degrade with each additional device in the chain.

## Flash Card # 139

**Ethernet Cable:**

- **Type:** Twisted Pair
- **Description:** Commonly used for wired Ethernet networks, consisting of twisted pairs of copper wires encased in an outer insulation jacket.
- **Variants:** Cat5e, Cat6, Cat6a, Cat7
- **Advantages:** Cost-effective, easy to install, supports high-speed data transmission.

 

- **Disadvantages:** Susceptible to electromagnetic interference, limited distance for transmission.

**Flash Card # 140**

**Fiber Optic Cable:**

- **Type:** Optical Fiber
- **Description:** Transmits data using light signals through thin strands of glass or plastic fibers.
- **Variants:** Single-mode, Multimode
- **Advantages:** High bandwidth, immune to electromagnetic interference, supports long-distance transmission.
- **Disadvantages:** More expensive than Ethernet cables, requires specialized equipment for installation and maintenance.

**Flash Card # 141**

**Coaxial Cable:**

- **Type:** Coaxial
- **Description:** It consists of a central conductor surrounded by a dielectric insulator, a metallic shield, and an outer insulating layer.
- **Variants:** RG-6, RG-59
- **Advantages:** Supports higher bandwidth than twisted pair cables, suitable for long-distance transmission.
- **Disadvantages:** Less flexible than twisted pair cables, more susceptible to signal degradation over long distances.

 

## Flash Card # 142

**Serial Cable:**

- **Type:** Serial
- **Description:** Connects devices using serial communication protocols, transmitting data bit by bit over a single wire.
- **Variants:** RS-232, RS-485
- **Advantages:** Simple and reliable, suitable for connecting devices over short distances.
- **Disadvantages:** Limited data transmission speed, prone to signal interference and noise.

## Flash Card # 143

**USB Cable:**

- **Type:** Universal Serial Bus (USB)
- **Description:** Connects peripheral devices, such as keyboards, mice, printers, and storage devices, to a computer or other host device.
- **Variants:** USB-A, USB-B, USB-C
- **Advantages:** Versatile, supports hot-swapping, provides power and data transfer capabilities.
- **Disadvantages:** Limited cable length for data transmission, compatibility issues with older devices.

## Flash Card # 144

**HDMI Cable:**

- **Type:** High-Definition Multimedia Interface (HDMI)
- **Description:** Transmits high-definition audio and video signals between multimedia devices, such as TVs, monitors, and gaming consoles.

 

- **Variants:** HDMI Standard, HDMI High Speed, HDMI Premium High Speed
- **Advantages:** Supports high-definition video and audio formats, easy to use with plug-and-play functionality.
- **Disadvantages:** Limited cable length for optimal signal quality, relatively high cost compared to other cables.

## Flash Card # 145

**Power Cable:**

- **Type:** Power Cord
- **Description:** Supplies electrical power from a power outlet to electronic devices, such as computers, monitors, and appliances.
- **Variants:** NEMA, IEC, CEE
- **Advantages:** Provides essential power supply for devices to operate, available in various lengths and configurations.
- **Disadvantages:** Limited flexibility for cable routing, may require surge protectors or UPS devices for added protection.

## Flash Card # 146

**RJ45 Connector:**

- **Type:** Modular Connector
- **Description:** Used with Ethernet cables to connect network devices, such as computers, routers, and switches.
- **Variants:** 8P8C (8 positions, 8 contacts)
- **Advantages:** Standardized connector for Ethernet networking, supports high-speed data transmission.
- **Disadvantages:** Requires proper crimping and termination for reliable connections, susceptible to damage if mishandled.

 

## Flash Card # 147

**Patch Cable:**

- **Type:** Twisted Pair
- **Description:** Short Ethernet cables with RJ45 connectors used to connect network devices in a local area network (LAN) or to connect devices to a patch panel.
- **Variants:** Cat5e, Cat6, Cat6a, Cat7
- **Advantages:** Provides flexibility for temporary or permanent network connections, available in various lengths and colors for easy identification.
- **Disadvantages:** Limited distance for data transmission, may require frequent replacement in high-traffic environments.

## Flash Card # 148

**Patch Panel:**

- **Type:** Networking Hardware
- **Description:** Mounted hardware used to organize and manage network connections by providing ports for connecting incoming and outgoing Ethernet cables.
- **Variants:** Loaded (with ports) or unloaded (without ports)
- **Advantages:** Simplifies cable management, facilitates easy connection and disconnection of network devices, reduces cable clutter.
- **Disadvantages:** Requires proper labeling and documentation for efficient troubleshooting, initial setup may be time-consuming.

## Flash Card # 149

**SFP (Small Form-factor Pluggable) Transceiver:**

- **Type:** Optical Transceiver Module

 

- **Description:** Plug-in module used in network switches and routers to convert electrical signals into optical signals for transmission over fiber optic cables, and vice versa.
- **Variants:** SFP, SFP+, QSFP, QSFP28
- **Advantages:** Modular design allows for easy replacement and upgrading supports various data rates and distances.
- **Disadvantages:** Higher cost compared to traditional fixed ports, requires compatible equipment for proper functionality.

**Flash Card # 150**

**Console Cable:**

- **Type:** Serial
- **Description:** Connects a computer or terminal to the console port of a networking device, such as a router or switch, for out-of-band management and configuration.
- **Variants:** RS-232
- **Advantages:** Enables direct access to the device's command-line interface (CLI) for configuration and troubleshooting, useful for initial setup and recovery.
- **Disadvantages:** Limited to local access, requires physical proximity to the device, may not be available on all devices.

**Flash Card # 151**

**TNC (Threaded Neill-Concelman) Connector:**

- **Type:** Coaxial
- **Description:** Screw-on connector used with coaxial cables to terminate RF (radio frequency) signals in applications such as Wi-Fi antennas and satellite communications.
- **Variants:** TNC, Reverse TNC (RP-TNC)

 

- **Advantages:** Provides secure and reliable connections, suitable for high-frequency applications, easy to install and remove.
- **Disadvantages:** Bulkier compared to other coaxial connectors, limited availability in certain regions.

## Flash Card # 152

**Thunderbolt Cable:**

- **Type:** Data Transfer
- **Description:** High-speed data transfer cable used to connect peripheral devices, such as external hard drives, monitors, and docking stations, to computers and laptops with Thunderbolt ports.
- **Variants:** Thunderbolt 1, Thunderbolt 2, Thunderbolt 3 (USB-C)
- **Advantages:** Offers fast data transfer speeds, supports daisy-chaining of multiple devices, and provides power delivery and video output capabilities.
- **Disadvantages:** Higher cost compared to other cable types, compatibility issues with non-Thunderbolt devices.

## Flash Card # 153

**SC (Subscriber Connector) Connector:**

- **Type:** Optical Fiber
- **Description:** Push-pull connector used with fiber optic cables to terminate optical signals in telecommunications and networking equipment.
- **Variants:** SC, SC/APC (Angled Physical Contact)
- **Advantages:** Provides low insertion loss and high return loss, easy to install and remove, suitable for high-density fiber optic installations.
- **Disadvantages:** Vulnerable to damage if mishandled, requires proper cleaning and inspection to maintain signal integrity.

 

## Flash Card # 154

**DVI (Digital Visual Interface) Cable:**

- **Type:** Video Interface
- **Description:** Connects digital display devices, such as monitors and projectors, to computers and video sources for high-quality video transmission.
- **Variants:** DVI-D (Digital), DVI-I (Digital and Analog), DVI-A (Analog)
- **Advantages:** Supports high-resolution video and digital audio transmission, available in single-link and dual-link configurations.
- **Disadvantages:** Limited compatibility with newer display interfaces, such as HDMI and DisplayPort.

## Flash Card # 155

**VGA (Video Graphics Array) Cable:**

- **Type:** Video Interface
- **Description:** Connects analog video display devices, such as monitors and projectors, to computers and video sources.
- **Variants:** VGA, SVGA, XGA
- **Advantages:** Widely compatible with older display devices, supports resolutions up to 1920x1080 pixels.
- **Disadvantages:** Limited color depth and image quality compared to digital interfaces like HDMI and DisplayPort.

## Flash Card # 156

**RJ11 Connector:**

- **Type:** Modular Connector
- **Description:** Used for telephone and DSL (Digital Subscriber Line) connections, typically with twisted pair cables.

 

- **Variants:** 6P2C (6 positions, 2 contacts), 6P4C (6 positions, 4 contacts)
- **Advantages:** Simple and easy to install, widely used for residential and small business telephone wiring.
- **Disadvantages:** Limited to voice and low-speed data transmission, not suitable for high-speed internet connections.

## Flash Card # 157

**Power over Ethernet (PoE) Cable:**

- **Type:** Ethernet Cable
- **Description:** Delivers electrical power and data signals over a single Ethernet cable, eliminating the need for separate power supplies for devices like IP cameras, VoIP phones, and wireless access points.
- **Variants:** IEEE 802.3af (PoE), IEEE 802.3at (PoE+), IEEE 802.3bt (PoE++)
- **Advantages:** Simplifies installation and reduces cable clutter, enables remote powering of devices in locations without electrical outlets.
- **Disadvantages:** Limited power delivery capacity, may require PoE-compatible devices and switches.

## Flash Card # 158

**DisplayPort Cable:**

- **Type:** Video Interface
- **Description:** Connects computers and multimedia devices to high-resolution display monitors and screens.
- **Variants:** DisplayPort 1.1, DisplayPort 1.2, DisplayPort 1.4

 

- **Advantages:** Supports high-resolution video and audio transmission offers multi-stream transport for daisy-chaining displays.
- **Disadvantages:** Less common than HDMI, may require adapters for compatibility with older devices.

**Flash Card # 159**

**MPO (Multi-fiber Push-On) Connector:**

- **Type:** Optical Fiber
- **Description:** High-density fiber optic connector used in data centers and high-speed networks to connect multiple fibers simultaneously.
- **Variants:** MPO-12, MPO-24
- **Advantages:** Facilitates rapid deployment and scalability of fiber optic networks, and reduces cable congestion and installation time.
- **Disadvantages:** Requires precise alignment and cleaning for optimal performance, and may have higher initial costs.

**Flash Card # 160**

**HDMI (High-Definition Multimedia Interface) Connector:**

- **Type:** Audio/Video Interface
- **Description:** Transmits uncompressed high-definition video and audio signals between multimedia devices, such as TVs, gaming consoles, and Blu-ray players.
- **Variants:** HDMI 1.4, HDMI 2.0, HDMI 2.1
- **Advantages:** Provides high-quality audio and video transmission, supports 4K and 8K resolutions, offers audio return channel (ARC) and consumer electronics control (CEC) features.
- **Disadvantages:** Limited cable length for optimal signal quality, compatibility issues with older devices and cables.

 

**Flash Card # 161**

**Term:** Category (Cat) Rating for Cables

- **Cat5/Cat5e:** Commonly used for Ethernet networks supporting speeds up to 1Gbps.
- **Cat6:** Offers improved performance over Cat5e, supporting speeds up to 10Gbps over shorter distances.
- **Cat6a:** Shielded Cat6 cable designed for higher performance and crosstalk resistance, supporting 10Gbps over longer distances.

**Flash Card # 162**

**Term:** RJ-45 Connector

**Function:** Standardized modular connector used for terminating Ethernet cables to connect network devices.

**Flash Card # 163**

**Term:** Cable Crimping

**Function:** Process of attaching an RJ-45 connector to the end of a network cable using a crimping tool.

**Flash Card # 164**

**Term:** Patch Cable

**Function:** Short Ethernet cable used to connect network devices within a rack or cabinet.

 

**Flash Card # 165**
**Term:** Crossover Cable
**Function:** Special type of Ethernet cable is used to connect two similar devices directly (e.g., switch to switch) without the need for a crossover device.

**Flash Card # 166**
**Term:** Network Sniffer
**Function:** Software tool that captures and analyzes all network traffic on a specific segment for troubleshooting and security monitoring.

**Flash Card # 167**
**Term:** Port Mirroring
**Function:** Technique that copies network traffic from one port on a switch to another port for monitoring purposes.

**Flash Card # 168**
**Term:** Network Performance Monitoring Tools

- **Simple Network Management Protocol (SNMP):** Industry-standard protocol for collecting network device information and performance metrics.
- **NetFlow/sFlow:** Technologies for monitoring network traffic flow and identifying bottlenecks.

 

**Flash Card # 169**

**Term:** Troubleshooting Methodology

- **Identify the problem:** Clearly define the network issue and its symptoms.
- **Isolate the problem:** Narrow down the scope of the problem to a specific device or network segment.
- **Diagnose the problem:** Analyze the root cause of the issue using various tools and techniques.
- **Resolve the problem:** Implement a solution to fix the problem and restore network functionality.
- **Verify the solution:** Confirm that the implemented solution has resolved the issue and that network performance is restored.

**Flash Card # 170**

**Term:** Backup and Disaster Recovery

**Function:** Creating regular backups of network configuration and data and a disaster recovery plan to ensure quick recovery in case of outages or failures.

**Flash Card # 171**

**Term:** Collisions

**Function:** Occurs when multiple devices on a shared network segment (like a hub) transmit data simultaneously, corrupting the packets and requiring retransmission. This is a major issue in hubs and can be minimized in switches.

 

### Flash Card # 172
**Term:** Excessive Collisions

- **Cause:** Faulty cables, bad network interface cards (NICs), or too many devices on a shared segment.
- **Symptom:** Slow network performance, dropped connections, and high collision count on switch interfaces.
- **Solution:** Replace faulty cables, troubleshoot NICs, or consider network segmentation (using switches).

### Flash Card # 173
**Term:** Interface Errors
**Function:** Errors detected on a network interface, such as CRC (Cyclic Redundancy Check) errors indicating data corruption or framing issues.

### Flash Card # 174
**Term:** High Interface Errors

- **Cause:** Faulty cables, bad NICs, physical layer problems (e.g., loose connections), or excessive network congestion.
- **Symptom:** Packet loss, slow network performance, and high error count on switch interfaces.
- **Solution:** Replace faulty cables, troubleshoot NICs, check for physical integrity, or address network congestion.

### Flash Card # 175
**Term:** Duplex Mismatch
**Function:** Occurs when two connected devices operate in different duplex modes (half-duplex or full-duplex). In half-duplex, only one device can

 

transmit at a time, while full-duplex allows simultaneous transmission in both directions.

**Flash Card # 176**

**Term:** Symptoms of Duplex Mismatch

- Slow network performance, dropped connections, and excessive retransmissions.

**Flash Card # 177**

**Term:** Troubleshooting Duplex Mismatch

- Check the duplex settings on both devices and ensure they match (usually full-duplex for modern networks).
- Network devices can often be configured to auto-negotiate duplex mode.

**Flash Card # 178**

**Term:** Speed Mismatch

**Function:** Occurs when two connected devices are configured for different speeds (e.g., 10Mbps vs. 100Mbps). Data may be transmitted at a slower speed or cause errors.

 

**Flash Card # 179**

**Term:** Symptoms of Speed Mismatch

- Similar to duplex mismatch, including slow network performance and dropped connections.

**Flash Card # 180**

**Term:** Identifying Interface and Cable Issues

- Use network management tools to check interface statistics for errors, collisions, and discarded packets.
- Physically inspect cables for damage or loose connections.
- Consider testing cables with a cable tester to confirm functionality.

**Flash Card # 181**

**Term:** Cable Length Limitations

**Function:** Different cable types have limitations on how far they can transmit data reliably. Exceeding these limits can lead to signal degradation and errors.

**Flash Card # 182**

**Term:** Crosstalk

**Function:** Interference between adjacent cables caused by electromagnetic coupling. This can corrupt data signals and cause errors, especially in unshielded twisted-pair cables (UTP).

 

**Flash Card # 183**

**Term:** Near-End Crosstalk (NEXT)

**Function:** Crosstalk that occurs between the transmit and receive pairs within the same cable.

**Flash Card # 184**

**Term:** Power over Ethernet (PoE)

**Function:** Technology that allows delivering electrical power along with data over an Ethernet cable, eliminating the need for separate power supplies for certain devices (e.g., VoIP phones).

**Flash Card # 185**

**Term:** PoE Issues

- Faulty cables may not support PoE or deliver insufficient power.
- Incorrect PoE standards (e.g., PoE vs. PoE+) can cause compatibility issues with devices.

**Flash Card # 186**

**Term:** Electromagnetic Interference (EMI)

**Function:** External electromagnetic fields can interfere with data transmission on network cables, especially in environments with heavy machinery or electrical equipment.

 

**Flash Card # 187**

**Term:** Grounding Issues

**Function:** Improper grounding can introduce electrical noise and disrupt data signals on network cables.

**Flash Card # 188**

**Term:** Cable Management

**Function:** Proper cable organization and separation from potential sources of interference (power cables, fluorescent lights) can help minimize crosstalk and EMI issues.

**Flash Card # 189**

**Term:** Cable Testing Tools

- **Cable tester:** Verifies cable functionality, pin configuration, and length limitations.
- **Time Domain Reflectometry (TDR):** Tool is used to identify cable faults and pinpoint their location on the cable length.

**Flash Card # 190**

**Term:** Preventive Maintenance

**Function:** Regularly inspecting cables for damage, ensuring proper cable management, and following recommended cable lengths can help prevent interface and cable issues.

 

**Flash Card # 191**
**Term:** OSI Model (Open Systems Interconnection)
**Function:** A conceptual framework for network communication, defining seven layers with specific functionalities.

**Flash Card # 192**
**Term:** Layer 1: Physical Layer
**Function:** Deals with the physical transmission of data bits over a physical medium like cables or fiber. (e.g., RJ-45 connectors, cable types)

**Flash Card # 193**
**Term:** Layer 2: Data Link Layer
**Function:** Responsible for error-free data transmission on a network segment, including addressing (MAC addresses) and media access control (e.g., switches, Ethernet frames).

**Flash Card # 194**
**Term:** Layer 3: Network Layer
**Function:** Enables routing of data packets across networks using logical addressing (IP addresses) and routing protocols. (e.g., routers, IP packets)

 

**Flash Card # 195**

**Term:** Layer 4: Transport Layer

**Function:** Provides reliable data transfer between applications on different devices, including port numbers and flow control. (e.g., TCP, UDP)

**Flash Card # 196**

**Term:** Layer 5: Session Layer

**Function:** Establishes, manages, and terminates sessions between communicating applications.

**Flash Card # 197**

**Term:** Layer 6: Presentation Layer

**Function:** Handles data presentation and encryption/decryption.

**Flash Card # 198**

**Term:** Layer 7: Application Layer

**Function:** Provides network services to applications like file transfer, email, and web browsing. (e.g., HTTP, FTP, SMTP)

**Flash Card # 199**

**Term:** TCP (Transmission Control Protocol)

**Function:** Reliable, connection-oriented transport layer protocol that guarantees in-order delivery of data packets.

 

### Flash Card # 200

**Term:** UDP (User Datagram Protocol)

**Function:** Connectionless transport layer protocol that offers faster but less reliable data delivery without error checking.

### Flash Card # 201

**Term:** IP (Internet Protocol)

**Function:** Network layer protocol responsible for addressing and routing of data packets across networks using IP addresses.

### Flash Card # 202

**Term:** DHCP (Dynamic Host Configuration Protocol)

**Function:** Automatically assigns IP addresses and other configuration settings to devices on a network.

### Flash Card # 203

**Term:** DNS (Domain Name System)

**Function:** Translates human-readable domain names (like [invalid URL removed]) into machine-readable IP addresses.

### Flash Card # 204

**Term:** HTTP (Hypertext Transfer Protocol)

**Function:** Application layer protocol that defines how web browsers and web servers communicate.

 

**Flash Card # 205**
**Term:** HTTPS (Secure Hypertext Transfer Protocol)
**Function:** Secure version of HTTP that encrypts communication between web browsers and servers.

**Flash Card # 206**
**Term:** SSH (Secure Shell)
**Function:** Secure protocol for remote login and command-line access to network devices.

**Flash Card # 207**
**Term:** SNMP (Simple Network Management Protocol)
**Function:** Industry-standard protocol for managing network devices and collecting performance metrics.

**Flash Card # 208**
**Term:** FTP (File Transfer Protocol)
**Function:** Application layer protocol for transferring files between computers on a network.

**Flash Card # 209**
**Term:** SMTP (Simple Mail Transfer Protocol)
**Function:** Protocol used for sending and receiving email messages.

**Flash Card # 210**

**Term:** VPN (Virtual Private Network)

**Function:** Creates a secure encrypted tunnel over the internet, allowing remote users to connect to a private network.

**Flash Card # 211**

**Term:** BGP (Border Gateway Protocol)

**Function:** Routing protocol used between autonomous systems (AS) on the internet to exchange routing information and determine the best path for data delivery.

**Flash Card # 212**

**Term:** OSPF (Open Shortest Path First)

**Function:** Interior Gateway Protocol (IGP) used within a single network to calculate the shortest path for routing data packets between devices.

**Flash Card # 213**

**Term:** RIP (Routing Information Protocol)

**Function:** Another IGP commonly used in smaller networks for exchanging routing information and determining forwarding paths.

 

**Flash Card # 214**
**Term:** VLANs (Virtual Local Area Networks)
**Function:** Logical segmentation of a network into smaller broadcast domains, improving security and network performance. Requires VLAN tagging protocols like 802.1Q.

**Flash Card # 215**
**Term:** MPLS (Multiprotocol Label Switching)
**Function:** Advanced routing technique that utilizes labels for faster and more efficient data forwarding across networks, often used in carrier backbones.

**Flash Card # 216**
**Term:** QoS (Quality of Service)
**Function:** Techniques to prioritize and manage network traffic to ensure consistent performance for critical applications like voice and video conferencing. Protocols like DiffServ and MPLS can be used for QoS.

**Flash Card # 217**
**Term:** IPSec (IP Security)
**Function:** Suite of protocols that provide secure communication over IP networks by encrypting data packets and authenticating communicating parties.

 

**Flash Card # 218**

**Term:** RADIUS (Remote Authentication Dial-In User Service)

**Function:** Protocol for centralized authentication, authorization, and accounting (AAA) management for network access control.

**Flash Card # 219**

**Term:** WPA/WPA2 (Wi-Fi Protected Access)

**Function:** Security protocols for securing wireless networks, offering encryption and authentication mechanisms to protect against unauthorized access.

**Flash Card # 220**

**Term:** SNMPv3 (Simple Network Management Protocol Version 3)

**Function:** Secure version of SNMP that provides encryption, authentication, and privacy for managing network devices.

**Flash Card # 221**

**Compare TCP and UDP**

**Reliability:**

1. **TCP:** Provides reliable, connection-oriented communication.
    - Ensures that data packets are delivered in sequence and without errors.
    - Implements error detection, retransmission, and flow control mechanisms.
2. **UDP:** Provides unreliable, connectionless communication.

 

- Does not guarantee packet delivery, sequencing, or error detection.
- Offers minimal overhead and faster transmission but may result in lost or out-of-order packets.

**Flash Card # 222**

**Connection Establishment:**

1. **TCP:** Establishes a connection before data exchange using a three-way handshake.
    - Initiates communication with a SYN segment, receives acknowledgment (ACK), and confirms with a final ACK.
    - Supports full-duplex communication and maintains state information for each connection.
2. **UDP:** Does not establish a connection before data exchange.
    - Sends data packets without prior negotiation or acknowledgment.
    - Suitable for real-time applications and scenarios where connection overhead is undesirable.

**Flash Card # 223**

**Header Size:**

1. **TCP:** Has a larger header size compared to UDP.
    - TCP header includes fields for sequence numbers, acknowledgment numbers, window size, and checksum.
    - Additional overhead for reliability features and connection management.
2. **UDP:** Has a smaller header size compared to TCP.
    - UDP header includes source port, destination port, length, and checksum fields.

 

- Minimal overhead, making it more efficient for certain types of applications.

**Flash Card # 224**

**Flow Control:**

1. **TCP:** Implements flow control mechanisms to manage data transmission rates.
    - Adjusts the rate of data flow based on receiver's buffer capacity and network congestion.
    - Prevents overwhelm by regulating the pace of data transmission.
2. **UDP:** Does not provide flow control mechanisms.
    - Sends data at the maximum rate allowed by the network and receiver's capabilities.
    - May result in packet loss or congestion in congested networks.

**Flash Card # 225**

**Error Handling:**

1. **TCP:** Detects and handles errors using checksums, acknowledgments, and retransmissions.
    - Resends lost or corrupted packets until successful delivery is confirmed.
    - Ensures data integrity and reliability at the expense of increased latency.
2. **UDP:** Provides minimal error detection using checksums.
    - Does not retransmit lost packets or correct errors, leaving error handling to the application layer.
    - Offers lower latency but may result in occasional data loss or corruption.

 

## Flash Card # 226

**Usage Scenarios:**

1. **TCP:** Suitable for applications requiring reliable, ordered, and error-free data transmission.
    - Used for web browsing, email, file transfer (FTP), and streaming media.
    - Preferred for applications sensitive to data integrity and delivery, even at the cost of increased latency.
2. **UDP:** Suitable for real-time communication and applications where low latency is critical.
    - Used for online gaming, voice and video conferencing, streaming media (e.g., VoIP, IPTV), and DNS (Domain Name System).
    - Preferred for applications prioritizing speed and responsiveness over reliability and ordered delivery.

## Flash Card # 227

**Order of Delivery:**

1. **TCP:** Guarantees the order of delivery for data packets.
    - Ensures that data packets arrive at the destination in the same order they were sent.
    - Achieved through sequence numbers and acknowledgment mechanisms.
2. **UDP:** Does not guarantee the order of delivery for data packets.
    - Packets may arrive out of order at the destination.
    - Provides no sequencing or acknowledgment mechanisms, allowing for faster transmission.

 

## Flash Card # 228

**Congestion Control:**

1. **TCP:** Implements congestion control mechanisms to manage network congestion.
    - Adjusts the transmission rate based on network conditions and congestion signals.
    - Prevents network congestion and ensures fair sharing of network resources.
2. **UDP:** Does not provide built-in congestion control mechanisms.
    - Relies on the application to manage congestion and packet loss.
    - May contribute to network congestion if not properly managed by the application.

## Flash Card # 229

**Packet Size:**

1. **TCP:** Supports variable packet sizes, depending on the Maximum Segment Size (MSS) negotiated during the TCP handshake.
    - Segments are typically larger to optimize throughput and efficiency.
2. **UDP:** Limited to smaller packet sizes due to the absence of segmentation and reassembly.
    - Suitable for applications with strict size constraints or real-time requirements.

## Flash Card # 230

**Connection State:**

1. **TCP:** Maintains connection state information for each active session.

 

- Tracks the state of each connection, including open, closed, and established.
- Requires additional overhead and memory resources to manage connection state.

2. **UDP:** Stateless protocol with no connection state tracking.
    - Each UDP packet is treated independently and does not require connection setup or teardown.
    - Offers lower overhead but lacks features such as reliable delivery and congestion control.

## Flash Card # 231

**Transmission Efficiency:**

1. **TCP:** Generally less efficient in terms of transmission overhead and latency.
    - Reliability mechanisms and connection management require more network resources and processing power.
    - Provides higher assurance of data delivery and integrity, suitable for critical applications.
2. **UDP:** Generally more efficient in terms of transmission overhead and latency.
    - Offers lower overhead and faster transmission speeds, making it ideal for real-time applications and multimedia streaming.
    - Sacrifices reliability for speed, suitable for applications tolerant of occasional packet loss or out-of-order delivery.

 

## Flash Card # 232

**Header Fields:**

1. **TCP:** Contains several header fields such as source port, destination port, sequence number, acknowledgment number, window size, and checksum.
    - Each field serves a specific purpose related to connection establishment, data transmission, and error detection.
2. **UDP:** Contains fewer header fields compared to TCP, including source port, destination port, length, and checksum.
    - Provides minimal information necessary for packet routing and error checking, reducing overhead and improving efficiency.

## Flash Card # 233

**Connection-Oriented vs. Connectionless:**

1. **TCP:** Connection-oriented protocol that establishes a virtual connection before data transmission.
    - Ensures reliable and ordered delivery of data packets.
    - Provides flow control and congestion avoidance mechanisms.
2. **UDP:** Connectionless protocol that does not establish a connection before data transmission.
    - Sends data packets independently without acknowledgment or retransmission.
    - Offers minimal overhead and faster transmission speeds but lacks reliability.

 

### Flash Card # 234

**Acknowledgment Mechanism:**

1. **TCP:** Uses acknowledgment (ACK) packets to confirm the receipt of data packets.
   - Sender waits for ACK before sending the next packet to ensure reliable delivery.
   - Retransmits unacknowledged packets after a timeout period.
2. **UDP:** Does not use acknowledgment packets.
   - Sends data packets without waiting for acknowledgment or retransmission.
   - Suitable for real-time applications where occasional packet loss is acceptable.

### Flash Card # 235

**Timeout and Retransmission:**

1. **TCP:** Implements timeout and retransmission mechanisms to handle lost or delayed packets.
   - Sender sets a timeout period for ACK receipt and retransmits packets if ACK is not received within the timeout.
   - Ensures reliable delivery but may introduce latency and overhead.
2. **UDP:** Does not have built-in timeout and retransmission mechanisms.
   - Relies on the application layer to detect and handle packet loss or delay.
   - Offers lower latency but may result in incomplete data delivery under adverse network conditions.

 

## Flash Card # 236

**Port Numbers:**

1. **TCP:** Uses port numbers to identify the source and destination applications.
   - Each TCP packet contains source and destination port numbers in the header.
   - Enables multiplexing of multiple applications on the same IP address.
2. **UDP:** Also uses port numbers for application identification.
   - Each UDP packet includes source and destination port numbers.
   - Allows for the simultaneous operation of multiple applications on the same host.

## Flash Card # 237

**Overhead and Efficiency:**

1. **TCP:** Generally has higher overhead due to reliability mechanisms and connection management.
   - Consumes more network resources and processing power.
   - Provides robustness and reliability at the expense of efficiency.
2. **UDP:** Typically has lower overhead and higher efficiency.
   - Requires fewer resources and offers faster transmission speeds.
   - Suitable for time-sensitive applications where speed is prioritized over reliability.

 

**Flash Card # 238**

**Term:** IP Address

**Function:** A unique identifier assigned to a device on an IP network, consisting of four octets (bytes) represented in dotted decimal notation (e.g., 192.168.1.10).

**Flash Card # 239**

**Term:** Subnet Mask

**Function:** Defines the network and host portions of an IP address, determining the number of available devices on a subnet. Represented in dotted decimal notation (e.g., 255.255.255.0).

**Flash Card # 240**

**Term:** Subnetting

**Function:** Process of dividing a large network into smaller logical subnets, improving manageability and security. Achieved by borrowing bits from the host portion of the IP address.

**Flash Card # 241**

**Term:** Classful vs. Classless Addressing

- **Classful addressing:** Older method that assigned IP addresses based on fixed network and host bit lengths (classes A, B, C). Mostly deprecated but understanding can be helpful.
- **Classless Inter-Domain Routing (CIDR):** Modern method that uses a subnet mask to define the network and host portions more flexibly.

 

## Flash Card # 242

**Term:** Common Subnet Masks and Usable Hosts

- /24 network: 255.255.255.0 (usable hosts: 254)
- /25 network: 255.255.255.128 (usable hosts: 126)
- /26 network: 255.255.255.192 (usable hosts: 62)

## Flash Card # 243

**Term:** Verifying IP Configuration

- Use the ip addr show command on Linux/Unix-based systems or ipconfig on Windows to view assigned IP addresses, subnet masks, and default gateways.

## Flash Card # 244

**Term:** Configuring Static IP Address

- Use network configuration tools or command-line interfaces (e.g., ifconfig on Linux) to manually assign an IP address, subnet mask, and default gateway to a network interface.

## Flash Card # 245

**Term:** DHCP (Dynamic Host Configuration Protocol)

**Function:** Automatically assigns IP addresses and other configuration settings to devices on a network, reducing manual configuration tasks. Requires a DHCP server on the network.

 

### Flash Card # 246

**Term:** Calculating Subnet Mask and Available Hosts

- Use online subnet calculators or formulas to determine the subnet mask and number of usable hosts for a desired network size.

### Flash Card # 247

**Term:** Verifying Subnetting Configuration

- Use tools like ping to test connectivity between devices on the same subnet (should work) and devices on different subnets (may require routing configuration).

### Flash Card # 248

**Term:** Default Gateway

**Function:** Router IP address that acts as the gateway for devices on a subnet to access resources outside the local network.

### Flash Card # 249

**Term:** Broadcast Address

**Function:** Special IP address within a subnet that represents all devices on that subnet. Used for certain network operations like sending ARP requests. It's calculated by setting all host bits in the subnet mask to 1 (e.g., for a /24 network with subnet mask 255.255.255.0, the broadcast address is 255.255.255.255).

 

## Flash Card # 250

**Term:** Network Address

**Function:** First usable IP address in a subnet, determined by setting all host bits in the subnet mask to 0 (e.g., for a /24 network with subnet mask 255.255.255.0, the network address is 192.168.1.0).

## Flash Card # 251

**Term:** Valid and Invalid IP Addresses

- An IP address cannot be the network address or broadcast address of a subnet.
- Loopback address (127.0.0.1) is reserved for internal testing purposes.

## Flash Card # 252

**Term:** Subnet Mask Borrowing

**Function:** In complex network designs, it may be necessary to borrow additional bits from the host portion to create even smaller subnets. This reduces the number of usable hosts per subnet but allows for more granular control.

## Flash Card # 253

**Term:** VLSM (Variable Length Subnet Mask)

**Function:** Technique that allows using different subnet masks for different subnets within a larger network, optimizing the allocation of IP addresses based on specific subnet requirements.

## Flash Card # 254
**Term:** IPv4 Depletion
**Function:** Due to the limited pool of IPv4 addresses and the rapid growth of internet users and devices, IPv4 addresses are becoming increasingly scarce. This has led to the adoption of IPv6 as the next-generation internet protocol.

## Flash Card # 255
**Term:** IPv4 Migration Strategies
- **Network Address Translation (NAT):** Technique that allows multiple devices on a private network to share a single public IP address for internet access.
- **Carrier Grade NAT (CGN):** Large-scale NAT deployed by internet service providers (ISPs) to conserve public IP addresses for their customers.

## Flash Card # 256
**Term:** IPv6 Transition Mechanisms
- **Tunneling:** Encapsulating IPv6 packets within IPv4 packets for transmission over existing IPv4 infrastructure.
- **Dual Stack:** Running both IPv4 and IPv6 protocols concurrently on a network, allowing gradual migration.

## Flash Card # 257
**Term:** Benefits of IPv6

 

- Vastly larger address space compared to IPv4, eliminating concerns about address depletion.
- Simplified header structure for faster routing.
- Improved security features built-in.

**Flash Card # 258**

**Term:** Packet Sniffers

**Function:** Software tools that capture and analyze all network traffic on a specific network segment. They can be used to identify abnormal traffic patterns, diagnose connectivity issues, and detect security threats.

**Flash Card # 259**

**Term:** Capturing Packets with Wireshark

**Function:** Wireshark is a popular open-source packet sniffer that allows capturing and analyzing network traffic data on wired and wireless networks. It offers deep inspection of protocols, filtering capabilities, and expert analysis tools.

**Flash Card # 260**

**Term:** Troubleshooting with Packet Captures

- Analyze captured packets to identify errors, dropped packets, and communication issues between devices.
- Look for signs of unauthorized access attempts, malware activity, or unusual network traffic patterns.
- Correlate packet captures with other troubleshooting methods (e.g., ping tests, logs) for a comprehensive diagnosis.

 

**Flash Card # 261**

**Term:** Network Trace Tools

- Traceroute (tracert on Windows): Reveals the path a data packet takes to reach its destination, helping identify network route issues like hops with high latency or unreachable destinations.
- Mtr (available on Linux/Unix): Provides a more detailed view of the traceroute path, including packet loss and latency information for each hop.

**Flash Card # 262**

**Term:** Troubleshooting with Network Trace Tools

- Use traceroute to pinpoint where network connectivity issues might be occurring along the path.
- Identify bottlenecks or congested hops that are causing slow network performance.
- Mtr can help diagnose intermittent connectivity problems by showing variations in packet loss and latency.

**Flash Card # 263**

**Term:** Network Monitoring Tools

- **Simple Network Management Protocol (SNMP):** Allows collecting network device information and performance metrics like interface utilization, CPU usage, and error counters.
- **Network Performance Monitoring (NPM) tools:** Offer comprehensive dashboards and visualizations to monitor network health, identify performance bottlenecks, and detect potential issues proactively.

 

**Flash Card # 264**

**Term:** Syslog Messages

**Function:** Standardized messages generated by network devices for logging events, errors, and system information.

**Flash Card # 265**

**Term:** Analyzing Syslog Messages

- Network devices can be configured to send syslog messages to a central server for analysis.
- Syslog messages can provide valuable clues about network issues, device errors, and security events.
- Tools can be used to filter, aggregate, and analyze syslog messages for troubleshooting purposes.

**Flash Card # 266**

**Term:** Troubleshooting Methodology (Advanced)

- **Deep Dive Analysis:** Once the root cause is narrowed down, use advanced tools and techniques for detailed analysis (e.g., packet capture filters, protocol analysis in Wireshark, configuration review).
- **Documentation:** Document the troubleshooting process, identified issues, and implemented solutions for future reference and knowledge sharing.
- **Preventative Maintenance:** Regularly monitor network performance, review logs, and implement preventative measures to minimize future occurrences of similar problems.

 

### Flash Card # 267

**Term:** Advanced Troubleshooting Skills

- Familiarity with various network protocols and their behavior.
- Understanding of routing principles and troubleshooting techniques.
- Ability to interpret network logs, packet captures, and other diagnostic outputs.
- Strong analytical and problem-solving skills to identify the root cause of network issues.

### Flash Card # 268

**Term:** Firewalls (Stateful vs. Stateless)

- **Stateful firewalls:** Track connections and allow return traffic based on established sessions, offering more granular control.
- **Stateless firewalls:** Filter packets based on predefined rules without tracking connections, offering faster performance but less control.

### Flash Card # 269

**Term:** Intrusion Detection Systems (IDS) and Intrusion Prevention Systems (IPS)

- **IDS:** Monitors network traffic for suspicious activity and sends alerts, but doesn't actively block threats.
- **IPS:** Detects and actively blocks malicious traffic based on predefined security rules.

### Flash Card # 270

**Term:** Security Information and Event Management (SIEM)

 

**Function:** Centralized platform that collects security events from various sources (firewalls, IDS, logs) for correlation, analysis, and incident response.

**Flash Card # 271**

**Term:** Vulnerability Scanning and Penetration Testing

- **Vulnerability scanning:** Automated process to identify security weaknesses in systems and applications.
- **Penetration testing:** Ethical hacking simulation where authorized testers attempt to exploit vulnerabilities to assess network security posture.

**Flash Card # 272**

**Term:** Cryptographic Protocols

- **Secure Sockets Layer (SSL)/Transport Layer Security (TLS):** Encrypts communication between web browsers and servers to protect data in transit (HTTPS).
- **Virtual Private Networks (VPNs):** Encrypts data traffic over a public network like the internet, creating a secure tunnel for remote access.

**Flash Card # 273**

**Term:** Secure Coding Practices

- **Input validation:** Sanitize user input to prevent injection attacks (e.g., SQL injection, XSS).
- **Principle of least privilege:** Grant users only the minimum permissions needed to perform their tasks.

 

- **Regular security updates:** Patch systems and applications promptly to address known vulnerabilities.

## Flash Card # 274

**Term:** Social Engineering Attacks

**Function:** Techniques that manipulate people into revealing confidential information or clicking on malicious links, often through phishing emails or phone calls.

## Flash Card # 275

**Term:** Denial-of-Service (DoS) and Distributed Denial-of-Service (DDoS) Attacks

- **DoS:** Overwhelms a target system with traffic, making it unavailable to legitimate users.
- **DDoS:** Large-scale DoS attack launched from multiple distributed sources, making it harder to mitigate.

## Flash Card # 276

**Term:** Best Practices for Mitigating DoS/DDoS Attacks

- Utilize DDoS mitigation services that can filter and block malicious traffic.
- Implement rate limiting to restrict the number of connections from a single source.
- Regularly test and update DDoS response plans.

 

**Flash Card # 277**

**Term:** Network Security Standards and Frameworks

- **National Institute of Standards and Technology (NIST) Cybersecurity Framework:** Provides a voluntary framework for managing cybersecurity risks.
- **International Organization for Standardization (ISO) 27001:** Standard for information security management systems, outlining best practices for protecting information assets.

**Flash Card # 278**

**Term:** WPA3 (Wi-Fi Protected Access 3)

**Function:** Latest security protocol for wireless networks, offering improved encryption (using Suite-B cryptography) and stronger authentication mechanisms compared to WPA2.

**Flash Card # 279**

**Term:** WPA3 Features

- Stronger password hashing (using key derivation function) for increased resistance to brute-force attacks.
- Simultaneous Authentication of Equals (SAE): Secure handshake process that mitigates the risk of password capture during key exchange.
- Optional 192-bit Protected Management Frames (PMF): Encrypts management and control frames for better privacy.

 

### Flash Card # 280

**Term:** Open vs. Closed Wireless Networks

- **Open networks:** No encryption, anyone can connect, highly insecure.
- **Closed networks:** Require authentication (WEP, WPA, WPA2, WPA3) for access, offering varying levels of security.

### Flash Card # 281

**Term:** WEP (Wired Equivalent Privacy) Vulnerabilities

**Function:** Outdated and easily compromised security protocol for wireless networks. Not recommended for use due to weak encryption algorithms and susceptibility to cracking techniques.

### Flash Card # 282

**Term:** Rogue Access Points (APs)

**Function:** Unauthorized wireless access points that mimic legitimate networks, potentially intercepting traffic or launching man-in-the-middle attacks.

### Flash Card # 283

**Term:** Detecting Rogue Access Points

- Use wireless network scanners to identify unauthorized APs in the vicinity.
- Monitor DHCP logs for unfamiliar MAC addresses that might be associated with rogue devices.
- Configure network devices to detect and block unauthorized access attempts.

 

### Flash Card # 284

**Term:** Wireless Network Best Practices

- Use strong encryption (WPA2 or WPA3) with complex passwords.
- Enable MAC filtering (allowing only authorized devices) if supported by your router (limited effectiveness against spoofing attacks).
- Disable SSID broadcast to make your network less discoverable.
- Keep your router firmware up-to-date with security patches.
- Consider using a separate Guest network for visitors with limited access permissions.

### Flash Card # 285

**Term:** Wireless Intrusion Prevention Systems (WIPS)

**Function:** Specialized security systems dedicated to monitoring and protecting wireless networks. They can detect unauthorized access attempts, rogue APs, and malicious activity on the wireless network.

### Flash Card # 286

**Term:** 802.1X Port-Based Network Access Control (PNAC)

**Function:** Security protocol that can be used with wired and wireless networks to enforce user authentication before granting access to the network. Requires additional infrastructure like RADIUS servers.

### Flash Card # 287

**Term:** Wireless Mesh Networks

**Function:** Networks where wireless devices connect with each other in a decentralized fashion, often used to extend wireless coverage in challenging environments. Security considerations for mesh networks include managing encryption keys and ensuring secure communication between mesh nodes.

### Flash Card # 288

**Limited Public IPv4 Addresses:**

- **Description:** Due to the scarcity of public IPv4 addresses, there are not enough addresses to assign to every device connected to the internet.
- **Solution:** Private IPv4 addressing allows organizations to create their own private networks using non-routable IP addresses, conserving public IPv4 addresses for internet-facing devices.

### Flash Card # 289

**Security and Isolation:**

- **Description:** Using private IPv4 addresses helps isolate internal networks from the public internet, providing an added layer of security.
- **Solution:** Devices within the private network can communicate with each other using private IP addresses, but they are not directly accessible from the internet, reducing the risk of unauthorized access and attacks.

### Flash Card # 290

**Internal Network Structure:**

- **Description:** Organizations often have complex internal network structures with multiple subnets and devices.

 

- **Solution:** Private IPv4 addressing allows for the creation of hierarchical network architectures, where devices within the same organization can communicate with each other using private IP addresses, regardless of their physical location.

## Flash Card # 291

**Cost Savings:**

- **Description:** Acquiring public IPv4 addresses can be expensive, especially for organizations with large numbers of devices.
- **Solution:** By using private IPv4 addresses internally, organizations can avoid the costs associated with obtaining public IP addresses for every device, reducing overall expenses.

## Flash Card # 292

**Scalability:**

- **Description:** Private IPv4 addressing facilitates network expansion and growth without the need to acquire additional public IP addresses.
- **Solution:** Organizations can easily add new devices and subnets to their internal networks using private IP addresses, without requiring changes to their public IP address allocation.

## Flash Card # 293

**Network Address Translation (NAT):**

- **Description:** NAT allows multiple devices within a private network to share a single public IP address when accessing the internet.

- **Solution:** Private IPv4 addressing enables NAT to translate private IP addresses to a single public IP address, conserving public IPv4 addresses and facilitating internet access for internal devices.

**Flash Card # 294**
**IPv6 Transition:**

- **Description:** With the depletion of IPv4 addresses, the transition to IPv6 is becoming increasingly important.
- **Solution:** Private IPv4 addressing provides a temporary solution for organizations still using IPv4 while transitioning to IPv6, allowing them to continue operating internal networks without immediate reliance on IPv6 addresses.

**Flash Card # 295**
**Network Segmentation:**

- **Description:** Organizations often divide their networks into segments for better management and security.
- **Solution:** Private IPv4 addressing enables the creation of distinct network segments using private IP address ranges, allowing organizations to apply different security policies and access controls to each segment.

**Flash Card # 296**
**Compliance Requirements:**

- **Description:** Many industries have regulatory requirements that mandate the protection of sensitive data.

 

- **Solution:** Using private IPv4 addresses helps organizations comply with data privacy regulations by ensuring that internal network communications remain within controlled environments and are not exposed to external threats.

## Flash Card # 297

**Network Performance:**

- **Description:** Public IP addresses are subject to network congestion and routing inefficiencies on the internet.
- **Solution:** Private IPv4 addressing allows organizations to create internal networks with optimized routing and performance, ensuring faster communication between devices and applications.

## Flash Card # 298

**Remote Access:**

- **Description:** Organizations often provide remote access to internal resources for employees working remotely or on the go.
- **Solution:** Private IPv4 addressing enables secure remote access solutions such as VPN (Virtual Private Network), allowing authorized users to connect to the internal network using private IP addresses while maintaining security and privacy.

## Flash Card # 299

**Device Management:**

- **Description:** Organizations need to efficiently manage and monitor their network devices and resources.

- **Solution:** Private IPv4 addressing simplifies device management by providing a standardized addressing scheme for internal devices, making it easier to track and administer network assets.

**Flash Card # 300**

**Address Space Conservation:**

- **Description:** With the depletion of public IPv4 addresses, conserving address space has become essential.
- **Solution:** Private IPv4 addressing allows organizations to use reserved address ranges (e.g., 10.0.0.0/8, 172.16.0.0/12, 192.168.0.0/16) for internal networks, preserving public IPv4 addresses for external-facing services and devices.

**Flash Card # 301**

**High Availability:**

- **Description:** Organizations require high availability and fault tolerance for critical applications and services.
- **Solution:** Private IPv4 addressing facilitates the implementation of redundant network architectures and failover mechanisms, ensuring continuous availability of internal resources in the event of network failures or disruptions.

**Flash Card # 302**

**IP Address Conservation:**

- **Description:** As IPv4 addresses are limited and increasingly depleted, conserving public IP addresses has become crucial.

 

- **Solution:** Private IPv4 addressing allows organizations to utilize a single public IP address for multiple internal devices through NAT (Network Address Translation), reducing the demand for public IPv4 addresses.

## Flash Card # 303

**Network Security Policies:**

- **Description:** Organizations implement various security policies to protect their internal networks from unauthorized access and cyber threats.
- **Solution:** Private IPv4 addressing enables the enforcement of security policies by segregating internal network traffic from external networks, limiting exposure to potential attacks and vulnerabilities.

## Flash Card # 304

**Network Performance Optimization:**

- **Description:** Network performance can be affected by factors such as latency, bandwidth constraints, and routing inefficiencies.
- **Solution:** Private IPv4 addressing allows organizations to design and optimize internal networks for better performance by reducing latency, minimizing congestion, and optimizing routing paths.

## Flash Card # 305

**Support for Legacy Systems:**

- **Description:** Many organizations still rely on legacy systems and applications that are not compatible with IPv6.

 

- **Solution:** Private IPv4 addressing provides continued support for legacy systems while allowing organizations to gradually transition to IPv6-compatible technologies at their own pace.

## Flash Card # 306

**Virtualization and Cloud Computing:**

- **Description:** Virtualization and cloud computing have become integral components of modern IT infrastructures.
- **Solution:** Private IPv4 addressing facilitates the deployment of virtualized environments and cloud-based services by providing private IP addresses for virtual machines, containers, and cloud instances within internal networks.

## Flash Card # 307

**IP Address Reuse and Recycle:**

- **Description:** Public IPv4 addresses are a finite and valuable resource that needs to be managed efficiently.
- **Solution:** Private IPv4 addressing allows organizations to reuse and recycle internal IP addresses without the need to obtain additional public IP addresses, thereby maximizing the utilization of available address space.

## Flash Card # 308

**Network Privacy and Confidentiality:**

- **Description:** Organizations need to ensure the privacy and confidentiality of sensitive data transmitted over internal networks.

 

- **Solution:** Private IPv4 addressing helps maintain network privacy and confidentiality by segregating internal traffic from the public internet, reducing the risk of data interception and unauthorized access.

## Flash Card # 309

**Ease of Network Administration:**

- **Description:** Simplifying network administration tasks is essential for efficient network management.
- **Solution:** Private IPv4 addressing provides a standardized and hierarchical addressing scheme for internal networks, making it easier to manage and troubleshoot network devices, configure routing, and allocate IP addresses to new devices.

## Flash Card # 310

**Network Flexibility:**

- **Description:** Organizations require flexible network architectures to adapt to changing business needs and technological advancements.
- **Solution:** Private IPv4 addressing allows organizations to design and implement customized network topologies, subnets, and addressing schemes tailored to their specific requirements without relying on public IP address availability.

 

## Flash Card # 311

**Compliance with Network Policies:**

- **Description:** Organizations must adhere to internal policies and guidelines governing network configuration, access controls, and security measures.
- **Solution:** Private IPv4 addressing supports compliance efforts by enabling organizations to enforce network policies consistently across internal networks, ensuring adherence to regulatory requirements and industry standards.

## Flash Card # 312

**Network Segregation for Different Departments:**

- **Description:** Organizations often have multiple departments or business units that require separate network environments.
- **Solution:** Private IPv4 addressing facilitates network segregation by allowing organizations to assign distinct IP address ranges to different departments or business units, ensuring isolation and autonomy while maintaining centralized management.

## Flash Card # 313

**IP Address Management (IPAM):**

- **Description:** Effective IP address management is essential for efficient network operations and resource allocation.
- **Solution:** Private IPv4 addressing simplifies IP address management tasks by providing a controlled and manageable pool of IP addresses for internal networks, streamlining IP address assignment, tracking, and administration processes.

 

## Flash Card # 314

**Interoperability with Third-Party Services:**

- **Description:** Organizations may need to integrate their internal networks with third-party services, vendors, or partners.
- **Solution:** Private IPv4 addressing facilitates interoperability by providing a standardized addressing scheme that can be easily communicated and configured across different network environments, ensuring seamless connectivity and data exchange.

## Flash Card # 315

**Disaster Recovery and Redundancy:**

- **Description:** Organizations need robust disaster recovery and redundancy strategies to minimize downtime and data loss in the event of network failures or disasters.
- **Solution:** Private IPv4 addressing supports disaster recovery efforts by enabling organizations to replicate and backup internal network resources across geographically dispersed locations using private IP addresses, ensuring business continuity and data resilience.

## Flash Card # 316

**IPv4-to-IPv6 Transition Mechanisms:**

- **Description:** As IPv6 adoption increases, organizations may need transitional mechanisms to facilitate coexistence between IPv4 and IPv6 networks.
- **Solution:** Private IPv4 addressing can serve as a bridge during the IPv4-to-IPv6 transition by enabling organizations to deploy dual-stack networks that support both IPv4 and IPv6 protocols, ensuring compatibility and interoperability between legacy and next-generation networks.

 

## Flash Card # 317

**Dynamic Host Configuration Protocol (DHCP):**

- **Description:** DHCP is a network protocol used to dynamically assign IP addresses to devices on a network.
- **Solution:** Private IPv4 addressing complements DHCP by providing a pool of private IP addresses that DHCP servers can dynamically allocate to network devices, simplifying IP address assignment and management in dynamic network environments.

## Flash Card # 318

**Network Segmentation for Security Zones:**

- **Description:** Organizations implement security zones to enforce different levels of access controls and security policies.
- **Solution:** Private IPv4 addressing facilitates network segmentation into security zones by allowing organizations to assign separate IP address ranges to each zone, ensuring isolation and minimizing the impact of security breaches or unauthorized access.

## Flash Card # 319

**Mobile Device Management (MDM):**

- **Description:** Organizations manage mobile devices (e.g., smartphones, tablets) used by employees for work-related tasks.
- **Solution:** Private IPv4 addressing supports MDM efforts by providing a private network infrastructure for mobile devices to connect securely and access internal resources, ensuring compliance with organizational policies and protecting sensitive data.

 

**Flash Card # 320**

**Virtual Private Networks (VPNs):**

- **Description:** VPNs enable secure remote access to internal networks over the internet.
- **Solution:** Private IPv4 addressing is used in VPN implementations to assign private IP addresses to remote users and devices, establishing a secure tunnel for encrypted communication and ensuring privacy and confidentiality of data transmitted over public networks.

**Flash Card # 321**

**Quality of Service (QoS) Management:**

- **Description:** QoS mechanisms prioritize network traffic to ensure optimal performance for critical applications and services.
- **Solution:** Private IPv4 addressing facilitates QoS management by enabling organizations to classify and prioritize internal network traffic based on IP address ranges, ensuring that mission-critical applications receive sufficient bandwidth and latency requirements are met.

**Flash Card # 322**

**Remote Monitoring and Management (RMM):**

- **Description:** Organizations remotely monitor and manage network devices, servers, and endpoints for performance monitoring, troubleshooting, and maintenance.
- **Solution:** Private IPv4 addressing supports RMM activities by providing private network connectivity for remote monitoring and management tools, allowing IT administrators to access and control network assets securely from remote locations.

 

## Flash Card # 323

**Secure Shell (SSH) Access:**

- **Description:** SSH is a cryptographic network protocol used for secure remote access and administration of network devices and servers.
- **Solution:** Private IPv4 addressing is used to restrict SSH access to internal network devices by assigning private IP addresses to SSH-enabled devices, limiting access to authorized users within the organization's private network.

## Flash Card # 324

**Network Address Translation (NAT) Traversal:**

- **Description:** NAT traversal techniques enable communication between devices behind NAT devices (e.g., routers, firewalls) and external networks.
- **Solution:** Private IPv4 addressing facilitates NAT traversal by providing private IP addresses that can be translated to public IP addresses by NAT devices, allowing internal devices to communicate with external networks seamlessly.

## Flash Card # 325

**Software-Defined Networking (SDN):**

- **Description:** SDN is an approach to network management that abstracts network control and forwarding functions, enabling centralized management and programmability.
- **Solution:** Private IPv4 addressing supports SDN deployments by providing a standardized addressing scheme for SDN controllers and virtual network overlays, simplifying network configuration and automation tasks.

 

### Flash Card # 326
**IPv4 Address Exhaustion:**
- **Description:** The depletion of available public IPv4 addresses due to the exponential growth of internet-connected devices.
- **Solution:** Private IPv4 addressing alleviates the strain on public IP address pools by allowing organizations to use reserved address ranges for internal networks, conserving public IPv4 addresses for internet-facing devices.

### Flash Card # 327
**Network Address Translation (NAT):**
- **Description:** NAT is a technique used to map private IP addresses to public IP addresses and vice versa, enabling communication between devices on private and public networks.
- **Solution:** Private IPv4 addressing complements NAT by providing a pool of private IP addresses that can be translated to a single public IP address for external communication, enabling connectivity while preserving public IP address space.

### Flash Card # 328
**Scalability and Growth:**
- **Description:** Organizations need scalable network solutions that can accommodate future growth and expansion.
- **Solution:** Private IPv4 addressing enables scalability by allowing organizations to create internal networks with ample address space, accommodating the addition of new devices, subnets, and network segments as the organization grows.

 

### Flash Card # 329

**Network Virtualization:**

- **Description:** Network virtualization allows organizations to create virtualized network environments that are decoupled from physical hardware.
- **Solution:** Private IPv4 addressing facilitates network virtualization by providing a pool of private IP addresses that can be dynamically assigned to virtual machines, containers, and virtual network interfaces, enabling flexible and scalable network architectures.

### Flash Card # 330

**Intranet and Extranet Connectivity:**

- **Description:** Organizations may need to establish secure connections between internal networks (intranets) and external networks (extranets) for collaboration with partners, suppliers, or customers.
- **Solution:** Private IPv4 addressing supports intranet and extranet connectivity by enabling secure communication between internal and external networks using private IP addresses, ensuring data privacy and confidentiality.

### Flash Card # 331

**Legacy System Integration:**

- **Description:** Many organizations still rely on legacy systems and applications that are not compatible with modern network technologies.
- **Solution:** Private IPv4 addressing facilitates the integration of legacy systems by providing a standardized addressing scheme that can coexist with legacy protocols and architectures, ensuring seamless interoperability and communication.

 

### Flash Card # 332

**Network Performance Monitoring and Optimization:**

- **Description:** Organizations need to monitor and optimize network performance to ensure optimal operation and user experience.
- **Solution:** Private IPv4 addressing enables granular monitoring and optimization of internal networks by providing visibility into traffic patterns, congestion points, and performance bottlenecks, allowing organizations to implement targeted optimizations and improvements.

### Flash Card # 333

**Term:** IPv6 Address

**Function:** Unique identifier for a device on an IPv6 network, consisting of eight 4-digit hexadecimal groups separated by colons (e.g., 2001:db8:1234:1000::5efe).

### Flash Card # 334

**Term:** IPv6 Prefix

**Function:** Similar to a subnet mask in IPv4, the prefix defines the network portion of an IPv6 address and the number of available host addresses within that network. Represented in a combination of the address and a slash followed by the prefix length (e.g., 2001:db8:1234:1000:/64).

 

### Flash Card # 335

**Term:** Configuring Static IPv6 Address

**Function:** Manually assigning an IPv6 address, prefix length, and optionally a default gateway on a network interface using configuration tools or commands (e.g., ifconfig on Linux).

### Flash Card # 336

**Term:** Verifying IPv6 Configuration

**Function:** Use commands like ip addr show on Linux/Unix or ipconfig on Windows to view assigned IPv6 addresses, prefixes, and default gateways.

### Flash Card # 337

**Term:** Automatic IPv6 Configuration (Stateless)

**Function:** Devices can automatically obtain an IPv6 address, prefix information, and default gateway from a router using Neighbor Discovery Protocol (NDP). Requires router advertisement enabled.

### Flash Card # 338

**Term:** Verifying Automatic IPv6 Configuration

**Function:** Use commands like ip addr show on Linux/Unix to check for a link-local IPv6 address (starting with fe80 ::) and potentially a globally routable address assigned via stateless autoconfiguration.

 

### Flash Card # 339

**Term:** Router Advertisement (RA)

**Function:** Messages sent by routers on an IPv6 network to advertise their presence, prefix information, and other configuration parameters to devices.

### Flash Card # 340

**Term:** Enabling Router Advertisement

**Function:** Configure routers to send Router Advertisements periodically, allowing devices to automatically configure their IPv6 settings. This is typically enabled by default on most modern routers.

### Flash Card # 341

**Term:** EUI-64 Based Addressing

**Function:** Technique for automatically deriving an interface's globally unique IPv6 address based on its MAC address. Offers plug-and-play connectivity without manual configuration.

### Flash Card # 342

**Term:** Verifying IPv6 Connectivity

**Function:** Use tools like ping6 to test connectivity between IPv6-enabled devices. A successful ping confirms basic reachability across the network.

### Flash Card # 343

**Term:** Loopback Address

 

**Function:** Special IPv6 address (: 1) used for internal testing purposes, similar to 127.0.0.1 in IPv4.

**Flash Card # 344**

**Term:** IPv6 Subnetting

**Function:** While less common than in IPv4 due to the vast address space, IPv6 subnetting allows further dividing a network into smaller segments. It's achieved by borrowing bits from the interface identifier portion of the address.

**Flash Card # 345**

**Term:** SLAAC (Stateless Address Autoconfiguration) Parameters

**Function:** Router Advertisements can include additional parameters beyond prefix information, such as: * Default router lifetimes: Defines how long a device should consider the advertised router valid. * Prefix lifetimes: Defines how long a device should consider the advertised prefix valid. * Hop limit: Maximum number of routers a packet can traverse before being discarded.

**Flash Card # 345**

**Term:** DHCPv6 (Dynamic Host Configuration Protocol version 6)

**Function:** Similar to DHCP in IPv4, DHCPv6 dynamically assigns IPv6 addresses, prefixes, and other configuration settings to devices on a network. Requires a DHCPv6 server.

 

### Flash Card # 347

**Term:** Stateful vs. Stateless Autoconfiguration

- **Stateless autoconfiguration (SLAAC):** Most common method, devices derive their addresses from router advertisements without server interaction.
- **Stateful autoconfiguration (DHCPv6):** Offers more centralized management and additional configuration options compared to SLAAC.

### Flash Card # 348

**Term:** Privacy Extensions (Privacy Extensions for Stateless Address Autoconfiguration)

**Function:** To enhance privacy, IPv6 allows generating randomized interface identifiers that change periodically, making it harder to track devices.

### Flash Card # 349

**Term:** ICMPv6 (Internet Control Message Protocol version 6)

**Function:** Similar to ICMP in IPv4, ICMPv6 provides error reporting and diagnostic messages for IPv6 communication, including neighbor solicitation and advertisement messages used in autoconfiguration.

### Flash Card # 350

**Term:** Verifying IPv6 Routing

**Function:** Tools like traceroute6 can be used to trace the path of an IPv6 packet across the network, helping identify potential routing issues.

 

## Flash Card # 351

**Term:** Security Considerations for IPv6

- While the vast address space reduces the risk of address depletion, securing IPv6 networks requires attention to access control mechanisms, firewalls, and encryption protocols adapted for IPv6.
- Many security best practices from IPv4 networks still apply to IPv6.

## Flash Card # 352

**Term:** Future of IPv6

**Function:** As IPv4 addresses become scarce, IPv6 is the future standard for internet protocol addressing. Understanding its configuration, verification, and security aspects is crucial for network administrators.

## Flash Card # 353

**Term:** IPv6 Routing Protocols

**Function:** Similar to IPv4 routing protocols, IPv6 uses protocols to exchange routing information and determine the best path for data packets across networks. Common protocols include:

- RIPng (Routing Information Protocol next generation)
- OSPFv3 (Open Shortest Path First version 3)
- BGP (Border Gateway Protocol) with IPv6 support

## Flash Card # 354

**Term:** Neighbor Discovery Protocol (NDP)

**Function:** Essential protocol for IPv6 autoconfiguration and neighbor communication. It performs functions like:

- **Address resolution:** Mapping IPv6 addresses to MAC addresses.

 

- **Router discovery:** Devices learn about available routers on the network.
- **Prefix discovery:** Devices obtain prefix information for network segmentation.

### Flash Card # 355

**Term:** IPv6 Static Routing Configuration

**Function:** Manually configuring routing tables on devices to define specific paths for forwarding traffic to different networks.

### Flash Card # 356

**Term:** Dynamic Routing Protocols for IPv6

**Function:** Protocols like OSPFv3 and BGP automatically learn about network topology and exchange routing information with neighboring devices, allowing for dynamic adaptation to network changes.

### Flash Card # 357

**Term:** Verifying IPv6 Routing Protocols

**Function:** Tools like show ip route or show bgp neighbors on network devices can be used to view routing tables and neighbor information learned through routing protocols.

### Flash Card # 358

**Term:** Security Features in IPv6

- **Built-in support for IPsec:** Enables secure communication by encrypting and authenticating data packets at the IP layer.

 

- **Stateless Address Autoconfiguration (SLAAC) Privacy Extensions:** Enhance privacy by generating randomized interface identifiers that change periodically.
- **Improved firewall capabilities:** Firewalls can be configured to filter IPv6 traffic based on source and destination addresses, ports, and other criteria.

## Flash Card # 359

**Term:** IPv6 Security Best Practices

- Implement strong authentication and authorization mechanisms to control access to the network.
- Use firewalls with proper IPv6 filtering rules.
- Regularly update network devices and software with security patches.
- Monitor network activity for suspicious behavior.

## Flash Card # 360

**Term:** IPv6 Security Challenges

- Transitioning from IPv4 to IPv6 may introduce new vulnerabilities if security considerations are not addressed.
- The larger address space of IPv6 can make it more challenging to implement granular access control policies.

 

**Flash Card # 361**
**Term:** Secure Neighbor Discovery (SEND)
**Function:** An extension to NDP that provides cryptographic authentication for neighbor solicitation and advertisement messages, mitigating address spoofing attacks.

**Flash Card # 362**
**Term:** IPv6 and Network Virtualization
**Function:** IPv6 is well-suited for network virtualization environments due to its vast address space, making it easier to assign unique addresses to virtual machines and containers.

**Flash Card # 363**
**Term:** IPv6 Tunneling Mechanisms
**Function:** Techniques for transmitting IPv6 packets over IPv4 networks, used during the transition period or for specific scenarios. Common methods include:

- **6to4 Tunneling:** Encapsulates IPv6 packets within IPv4 packets for transmission over IPv4 infrastructure.
- **Teredo Tunneling:** Utilizes UDP encapsulation for IPv6 over IPv4.

**Flash Card # 364**
**Term:** IPv6 Troubleshooting Tools
**Function:** Similar to IPv4 troubleshooting, various tools can be used to diagnose issues in IPv6 networks:

- **ping6:** Tests basic reachability between IPv6-enabled devices.

 

- **traceroute6:** Reveals the path of an IPv6 packet across the network, helping identify routing problems.
- **tcpdump or wireshark:** Capture and analyze IPv6 traffic for detailed inspection of packet flow and potential errors.
- **ndp-proxy:** Simulates neighbor solicitation and advertisement messages to diagnose NDP-related issues.

## Flash Card # 365

**Term:** Troubleshooting IPv6 Autoconfiguration

- Verify if Router Advertisements are being sent by routers.
- Check if devices are obtaining valid IPv6 addresses and prefixes.
- Ensure firewall rules don't block Neighbor Discovery Protocol (NDP) traffic.
- Consider using static IPv6 configuration for troubleshooting purposes if autoconfiguration issues persist.

## Flash Card # 366

**Term:** Troubleshooting IPv6 Routing

- Use show ip route or show bgp neighbors commands to verify learned routes and neighbors in routing protocols.
- Utilize traceroute6 to pinpoint potential routing hops where packets might be dropped.
- Check firewall rules to ensure they don't block legitimate IPv6 traffic.
- Consult routing protocol logs for error messages or warnings.

 

**Flash Card # 367**

**Term:** Troubleshooting IPv6 Security Issues

- Analyze firewall logs for suspicious activity or dropped IPv6 packets.
- Verify proper authentication and authorization mechanisms are in place.
- Check for vulnerabilities in network devices and software and apply security patches promptly.
- Utilize tools like nmap (with IPv6 support) to scan for open ports and potential security weaknesses.

**Flash Card # 368**

**Term:** Advanced Troubleshooting Techniques

- **Packet capture analysis with tcpdump or wireshark:** Filter and analyze captured IPv6 traffic to identify specific issues like missing headers, invalid options, or dropped packets.
- **Network traffic visualization tools:** Can provide a graphical representation of IPv6 traffic flow and identify bottlenecks or congestion points.
- **Expert resources and communities:** Consulting with network specialists or online communities can offer valuable insights for complex troubleshooting scenarios.

**Flash Card # 369**

**Term:** Best Practices for IPv6 Troubleshooting

- **Follow a systematic approach:** Start with basic connectivity tests and gradually move towards more advanced diagnostics.
- **Document troubleshooting steps and findings:** Helps track progress and share information with others.

 

- **Stay updated on IPv6 technologies and troubleshooting techniques:** The IPv6 landscape is constantly evolving, so continuous learning is essential.

## Flash Card # 370

**Term:** Proactive Network Monitoring

- Implement network monitoring tools to identify potential issues before they significantly impact network performance or security.
- Regularly review logs and alerts from network devices and security solutions.
- Perform vulnerability scans and penetration testing to proactively detect security weaknesses.

## Flash Card # 371

**Term:** Importance of IPv6 Troubleshooting Skills

- As IPv6 adoption continues to grow, the ability to troubleshoot IPv6-related problems becomes increasingly crucial for network administrators.
- Effective troubleshooting skills minimize downtime, ensure network stability, and protect against security threats.

## Flash Card # 372

**Term:** The Future of IPv6 Troubleshooting

- Automation tools and machine learning techniques are emerging to assist with IPv6 network monitoring and troubleshooting.
- Staying informed about these advancements can help network professionals optimize their troubleshooting strategies.

 

### Flash Card # 373

**Term:** Continuous Learning

- The world of networking is constantly evolving. Dedicating time to learning about new tools, technologies, and best practices remains vital for successful IPv6 troubleshooting and network management.

### Flash Card # 374

**Unicast Address:**

- **Description:** Identifies a single interface within an IPv6 network.
- **Example:** 2001:0db8:85a3:0000:0000:8a2e:0370:7334
- **Purpose:** Used for one-to-one communication between devices.

### Flash Card # 375

**Multicast Address:**

- **Description:** Identifies a group of interfaces within an IPv6 network.
- **Example:** FF02::1
- **Purpose:** Used for one-to-many communication, where data is sent to multiple recipients simultaneously.

### Flash Card # 376

**Anycast Address:**

- **Description:** Identifies a group of interfaces, but the data is routed to the nearest interface in terms of routing distance.
- **Example:** 2001:0db8:85a3:0000:0000:8a2e:0370:7334
- **Purpose:** Used for distributed services where the closest instance of a service responds to the request.

 

### Flash Card # 377

**Loopback Address:**

- **Description:** Points back to the same device, allowing a device to send data to itself.
- **Example:**::1 (IPv6 equivalent of 127.0.0.1 in IPv4)
- **Purpose:** Used for testing network interfaces and applications on the local device.

### Flash Card # 378

**Link-Local Address:**

- **Description:** Used for communication within the same subnet or link.
- **Example:** FE80::1
- **Purpose:** Ensures communication between devices on the same local network segment without the need for a globally unique address.

### Flash Card # 379

**Global Unicast Address:**

- **Description:** Globally routable IPv6 addresses used for communication over the internet.
- **Example:** 2001:0db8:85a3:0000:0000:8a2e:0370:7334
- **Purpose:** Allows devices to communicate with each other across the internet using a unique global IPv6 address.

 

## Flash Card # 380

**Unique Local Address (ULA):**

- **Description:** Used for local addressing within a private network similar to IPv4 private addresses (e.g., 10.0.0.0/8, 192.168.0.0/16).
- **Example:** FD00::/8
- **Purpose:** Provides private addressing space for internal networks, ensuring uniqueness and privacy within the organization.

## Flash Card # 381

**IPv4-Compatible IPv6 Address:**

- **Description:** Represents an IPv4 address within an IPv6 address format.
- **Example:**::192.0.2.1 (for IPv4 address 192.0.2.1)
- **Purpose:** Facilitates the transition from IPv4 to IPv6 by allowing IPv6-only devices to communicate with IPv4-only devices.

## Flash Card # 382

**IPv4-Mapped IPv6 Address:**

- **Description:** Represents an IPv4 address embedded within an IPv6 address format.
- **Example:**:::FFFF:192.0.2.1 (for IPv4 address 192.0.2.1)
- **Purpose:** Enables IPv6-only applications to communicate with IPv4-only applications in a dual-stack environment.

 

### Flash Card # 383

**Documentation Address:**

- **Description:** Reserved for documentation and examples, not meant for actual use on a network.
- **Example:** 2001:0db8:0:0:0:0:0:1
- **Purpose:** Used in documentation, tutorials, and educational materials to illustrate IPv6 addressing concepts.

### Flash Card # 384

**Site-Local Address:**

- **Description:** Deprecated IPv6 address type intended for communication within an organization's network.
- **Example:** FEC0::1
- **Purpose:** Originally intended for local communication, but deprecated due to lack of global uniqueness and replaced by Unique Local Addresses (ULA).

### Flash Card # 385

**Global Aggregatable Address:**

- **Description:** An obsolete term referring to global unicast addresses in IPv6 that are globally routable and hierarchical.
- **Example:** 2001:0db8:85a3:0000:0000:8a2e:0370:7334
- **Purpose:** Originally used to emphasize the hierarchical structure of global IPv6 addresses, now simply referred to as global unicast addresses.

 

## Flash Card # 386

**Reserved Addresses:**

- **Description:** Addresses reserved for specific purposes and not assignable to devices or interfaces.
- **Example:** (Unspecified Address), ::1 (Loopback Address), FF00::/8 (Multicast Addresses), etc.
- **Purpose:** Serve special functions such as loopback testing, multicast communication, and addressing unspecified or all nodes on a network.

## Flash Card # 387

**Transient Addresses:**

- **Description:** Temporary IPv6 addresses used for communication that are short-lived and dynamically assigned.
- **Example:** Temporary addresses generated using privacy extensions (e.g., IPv6 Temporary Address)
- **Purpose:** Enhance privacy by changing frequently and making it harder for attackers to track devices over time.

## Flash Card # 388

**Stable Addresses:**

- **Description:** Long-term IPv6 addresses that remain consistent and are associated with a specific device or interface.
- **Example:** Permanent addresses assigned statically or using stateless address autoconfiguration (SLAAC).
- **Purpose:** Provide a stable identity for devices or interfaces within the network, facilitating communication and network management.

 

## Flash Card # 389

**Prefix-Delegation Address:**

- **Description:** IPv6 addresses assigned dynamically to network segments or devices by a router using Prefix Delegation (PD).
- **Example:** Addresses delegated to downstream routers or network segments from the global prefix.
- **Purpose:** Facilitates automatic address assignment and configuration in large IPv6 networks, ensuring efficient address management.

## Flash Card # 390

**Special-Purpose Addresses:**

- **Description:** Addresses reserved for specific uses or purposes defined by Internet Engineering Task Force (IETF) standards.
- **Example:** IPv6 addresses for 6to4 tunneling, Teredo tunneling, etc.
- **Purpose:** Support specialized network functions such as IPv6 transition mechanisms, tunneling, and protocol extensions.

## Flash Card # 391

**Unique Subnet Address:**

- **Description:** An IPv6 address that uniquely identifies a subnet within an IPv6 network.
- **Example:** Addresses allocated to individual subnets within a larger IPv6 network.
- **Purpose:** Enables hierarchical addressing and routing within IPv6 networks, ensuring efficient packet forwarding and network management.

 

### Flash Card # 392

**Broadcast Address:**

- **Description:** An address used to broadcast packets to all devices on a network.
- **Example:** There is no broadcast address in IPv6; multicast addresses are used instead.
- **Purpose:** Broadcast communication is deprecated in IPv6 in favor of more efficient multicast communication.

### Flash Card # 393

**IPv6 Link-Local Unicast Address:**

- **Description:** An address used for communication within the same network segment.
- **Example:** FE80::1
- **Purpose:** Ensures communication between devices on the same link without the need for a globally unique address.

### Flash Card # 394

**IPv6 Unique Local Unicast Address (ULA):**

- **Description:** An address used for private communication within an organization.
- **Example:** FD00::1
- **Purpose:** Provides a private addressing scheme for internal networks, similar to IPv4 private addresses (e.g., 192.168.x.x).

 

## Flash Card # 395

**IPv6 Solicited-Node Multicast Address:**

- **Description:** An address used for Neighbor Discovery Protocol (NDP) and Address Resolution Protocol (ARP) in IPv6.
- **Example:** FF02::1:FF00:0/104 + (Last 24 bits of the unicast address)
- **Purpose:** Enables efficient address resolution and neighbor discovery in IPv6 networks.

## Flash Card # 396

**IPv6 Anycast Address:**

- **Description:** An address used to route packets to the nearest interface within a group of devices.
- **Example:** ::1
- **Purpose:** Facilitates load balancing and fault tolerance by directing traffic to the closest available instance of a service.

## Flash Card # 397

**IPv6 Global Unicast Address:**

- **Description:** An address used for communication over the internet in IPv6.
- **Example:** 2001:0db8:85a3:0000:0000:8a2e:0370:7334
- **Purpose:** Allows devices to communicate with each other across the internet using unique global IPv6 addresses.

 

## Flash Card # 398

**IPv6 Teredo Address:**

- **Description:** An IPv6 address used in Teredo tunneling for IPv6 connectivity over IPv4 networks.
- **Example:** 2001::/32
- **Purpose:** Enables IPv6 communication over IPv4 networks by encapsulating IPv6 packets within IPv4 packets.

## Flash Card # 399

**IPv6 6to4 Address:**

- **Description:** An IPv6 address used in 6to4 tunneling for automatic IPv6 connectivity between IPv6 networks over an IPv4 network.
- **Example:** 2002::/16
- **Purpose:** Facilitates the transition from IPv4 to IPv6 by allowing automatic tunneling between IPv6 networks over IPv4 networks.

## Flash Card # 400

**IPv6 Documentation Address:**

- **Description:** A reserved IPv6 address used for documentation and examples.
- **Example:** 2001:db8::/32
- **Purpose:** Used in documentation, tutorials, and educational materials to illustrate IPv6 addressing concepts and scenarios.

 

## Flash Card # 401

**Term:** Verifying IP Parameters

**Function:** Ensuring a device on a network has a valid IP address, subnet mask, default gateway, and DNS server addresses configured correctly. This allows the device to communicate with other devices and access the internet.

## Flash Card # 402

**Windows:**

- **Command:** ipconfig
- **Output:** Displays details like IP address, subnet mask, default gateway, DHCP server, and DNS servers.
- **Additional Information:** Use ipconfig /all for more details on network adapters and leases.

## Flash Card # 403

**Mac OS:**

- **Method 1:** System Preferences > Network > Select Network Interface > Advanced > TCP/IP > Configure IPv4 (or IPv6) > Click "Renew DHCP Lease" or manually configure details.
- **Method 2:** Terminal Command: ifconfig
- **Output:** Displays information on network interfaces, including IP address, subnet mask, and MAC address.

## Flash Card # 404

**Linux:**

- **Command:** ip addr show

 

- **Output:** Lists all network interfaces and their associated IP addresses, subnet masks, and MAC addresses.
- **Additional Information:** Use route -n to view the routing table and default gateway.

## Flash Card # 405

**Common Verification Points:**

- **IP Address:** Is it a valid IP address within the network range (not a private address like 10.0.0.1 or 192.168.1.1 used on most home networks)?
- **Subnet Mask:** Does it correctly define the network and host portions for your network configuration?
- **Default Gateway:** Is it the correct IP address of the router or gateway device that directs traffic outside the local network?
- **DNS Servers:** Are valid DNS server addresses configured to resolve domain names to IP addresses (e.g., 8.8.8.8, 1.1.1.1)?

## Flash Card # 406

**Troubleshooting Tips:**

- If IP parameters are not obtained automatically (DHCP), consider manually configuring them.
- Use online subnet mask calculators to determine the network range and available addresses based on your subnet mask.
- Check the router configuration if the default gateway seems incorrect.
- Consult network documentation or your internet service provider (ISP) for recommended DNS server settings.

 

## Flash Card # 407

**Additional Tools:**

- Network configuration tools (built-in to operating systems)
- Third-party IP scanner software
- Router configuration interface

## Flash Card # 408

**Benefits of Verifying IP Parameters:**

- Ensures proper network connectivity and internet access.
- Helps diagnose network troubleshooting issues.
- Maintains network security by ensuring devices have valid IP addresses within the designated network range.

## Flash Card # 409

**Remember:**

- Different versions of Windows, Mac OS, and Linux may have slight variations in commands or interfaces.
- Always consult your specific operating system documentation for detailed instructions.

## Flash Card # 410

**Advanced Verification:**

- Use tools like ping to test connectivity to specific devices or IP addresses.
- Analyze routing tables for proper network path configuration.
- For complex network troubleshooting, consider network monitoring tools and advanced diagnostics.

 

## Flash Card # 411

**Term:** DHCP Lease Information

**Function:** When using DHCP (Dynamic Host Configuration Protocol) for automatic IP assignment, verify the lease information displayed by ipconfig (Windows) or ip addr show (Linux). This includes:

- **Lease Obtained:** Time when the IP address was assigned to the device.
- **Lease Expires:** Time when the IP address lease expires, requiring renewal.

## Flash Card # 412

**Troubleshooting Automatic IP Assignment:**

- If DHCP isn't assigning an IP address:
  - Check if DHCP is enabled on the network router.
  - Verify network cable connection and functionality.
  - Release and renew the DHCP lease using commands or network settings.
  - Consider manually configuring a static IP address if DHCP continues to fail.

## Flash Card # 413

**Subnet Mask Issues:**

- An incorrect subnet mask can lead to connectivity problems. Ensure the subnet mask matches the network configuration, defining the network and host portions accurately.
- Use online subnet mask calculators or consult network documentation to determine the correct subnet mask for your network.

 

## Flash Card # 414

**Default Gateway Issues:**

- An incorrect default gateway can prevent internet access. Verify the default gateway matches the IP address of your router or network gateway device.
- Consult router documentation or network settings to confirm the correct default gateway address.

## Flash Card # 415

**DNS Server Issues:**

- Incorrect or unresponsive DNS servers can prevent domain name resolution. Verify valid DNS server addresses are configured.
- Use public DNS servers like 8.8.8.8 (Google) or 1.1.1.1 (Cloudflare) as alternatives if your ISP's DNS servers are unresponsive.

## Flash Card # 416

**Advanced Troubleshooting Tools:**

- **ping:** Tests basic connectivity to specific IP addresses or hostnames.
- **traceroute (or tracert on Windows):** Reveals the path packets take to reach a destination, helping identify bottlenecks or routing issues.
- **arp (Address Resolution Protocol):** Displays the ARP cache, mapping IP addresses to MAC addresses, useful for network troubleshooting.

 

## Flash Card # 417

**Network Monitoring Tools:**

- Provide real-time insights into network performance, including IP configuration details for connected devices.
- Can generate alerts for potential issues like IP conflicts or abnormal network traffic.
- Offer features like device discovery, bandwidth monitoring, and traffic analysis.

## Flash Card # 418

**Static vs. Dynamic IP Configuration:**

- **Static IP:** Manually assigning a fixed IP address, subnet mask, default gateway, and DNS servers to a device. Offers more control but requires manual configuration for each device.
- **Dynamic IP (DHCP):** Automatically obtains IP parameters from a DHCP server. More convenient for large networks but may require troubleshooting if DHCP fails.

## Flash Card # 419

**Best Practices for IP Verification:**

- Regularly verify IP parameters, especially on critical devices like servers.
- Document IP configurations for reference and troubleshooting purposes.
- Standardize IP configuration settings for easier network management.
- Implement DHCP reservations for essential devices to ensure they always receive the same IP address.

 

## Flash Card # 420

**Security Considerations:**

- Avoid using private IP addresses (ranges like 10.0.0.0/8 or 192.168.0.0/16) on devices connected directly to the internet, as they might conflict with internal network addressing schemes.
- Use strong passwords for router access and consider network segmentation to improve security if applicable.

## Flash Card # 421

**Term:** Network Interface Card (NIC) Drivers

**Function:** Software that allows the operating system to communicate with the physical network adapter (NIC) hardware. Updated drivers ensure compatibility and optimal network performance.

## Flash Card # 422

**Troubleshooting NIC Driver Issues:**

- Network connectivity problems can be caused by outdated, corrupted, or incompatible NIC drivers.
- Update NIC drivers through operating system update mechanisms or by downloading them from the manufacturer's website.
- Check device manager (Windows) or system logs (Linux/Mac) for errors related to NIC drivers.

 

## Flash Card # 423

**Network Configuration Files:**

- Different operating systems use configuration files to store network settings like IP addresses, subnet masks, and routing information.
- Understanding these files (e.g., /etc/network/interfaces in Linux) can be helpful for advanced troubleshooting.
- Editing these files with caution is recommended, as mistakes can disrupt network connectivity.

## Flash Card # 424

**Firewall Rules:**

- Firewalls can block legitimate network traffic if not configured correctly.
- Verify firewall rules allow necessary communication for the device's intended purpose.
- Consult network security policies and firewall documentation for proper configuration.

## Flash Card # 425

**Network Security Groups (NSGs) - Cloud Environments**

- Cloud platforms like Azure or AWS utilize NSGs to control network traffic flow between resources.
- Misconfigured NSGs can restrict communication and prevent applications from functioning correctly.
- Review NSG rules and ensure they allow necessary inbound and outbound traffic for your cloud resources.

 

## Flash Card # 426

**Packet Capture Analysis (Advanced):**

- Tools like tcpdump (Linux/Unix) or Wireshark can capture network traffic data for in-depth analysis.
- Analyze packet headers for source and destination IP addresses, protocols used, and potential errors.
- Utilize filters to focus on specific network traffic of interest.

## Flash Card # 427

**Network Protocol Analysis:**

- Understanding protocols like TCP/IP, UDP, and DNS can help diagnose communication issues.
- Analyze captured packets to identify issues like missing acknowledgments, dropped packets, or protocol errors.
- Consult network protocol documentation for detailed information on specific protocols.

## Flash Card # 428

**Routing Table Interpretation:**

- The routing table shows how the device routes network traffic to different destinations.
- Analyze the routing table to identify the default gateway and network routes.
- Incorrect routing table entries can lead to connectivity problems.

 

## Flash Card # 429

**Advanced Troubleshooting Techniques:**

- Kernel logs (Linux/Unix) or system event logs (Windows) can provide valuable clues about network-related errors or warnings.
- Utilize network performance monitoring tools to analyze network traffic patterns and identify bottlenecks or anomalies.
- Consult online resources and communities for troubleshooting specific network issues or error messages.

## Flash Card # 430

**Importance of Understanding OS Internals:**

- A deeper understanding of network configuration files, routing mechanisms, and network protocol behavior within the operating system empowers network professionals to diagnose and resolve complex network issues more effectively.

## Flash Card # 431

**Term:** Software-Defined Networking (SDN)

**Function:** SDN decouples the data plane (packet forwarding) from the control plane (network programming) offering centralized network management and programmability.

## Flash Card # 432

**IP Verification in SDN Environments:**

- SDN controllers manage IP address assignment and configuration through APIs.

 

- Tools provided by the SDN controller or OpenFlow switches can be used to verify IP configurations for virtual machines or containers.

**Flash Card # 433**
**Network Function Virtualization (NFV):**
**Function:** NFV virtualizes network functions like firewalls, load balancers, and intrusion detection systems, offering flexibility and scalability.

**Flash Card # 434**
**IP Verification in NFV Environments:**

- IP verification procedures may involve checking configurations within virtual network functions (VNFs) managed by the NFV orchestrator.

**Flash Card # 435**
**Containerization and IP Management:**

- Container technologies like Docker utilize container networking to assign IP addresses to containers.
- Docker network commands or tools provided by the container orchestration platform can be used to verify IP configurations for containers.

 

## Flash Card # 436
**IP Verification in Cloud-Native Environments:**
- Cloud platforms like AWS or Azure use various mechanisms for IP address management.
- Cloud console interfaces, APIs, or command-line tools can be used to verify IP configurations for cloud resources like virtual machines or containers.

## Flash Card # 437
**IPv6 Adoption and Verification Challenges:**
- The vast address space of IPv6 introduces new challenges for verifying IP configurations, especially in mixed IPv4/IPv6 environments.
- Network administrators need to be familiar with IPv6 specific tools and verification techniques.

## Flash Card # 438
**Emerging Network Technologies and IP Management:**
- Technologies like Intent-Based Networking (IBN) aim to automate network configuration and management, potentially impacting IP verification procedures.
- Staying updated on emerging technologies and their impact on IP management is crucial for network professionals.

## Flash Card # 439
**Security Considerations in IP Verification:**

 

- Verifying IP configurations is not just about functionality, but also about security.
- Ensure proper access controls are in place to prevent unauthorized modification of IP configurations.
- Consider using tools that can detect and report suspicious changes to IP settings.

## Flash Card # 440

**The Future of IP Verification:**

- Automation and orchestration tools are likely to play a more significant role in IP verification, especially in large and complex networks.
- Network professionals will need to adapt to new tools and methodologies for efficient IP verification in evolving network environments.

## Flash Card # 441

**Radio Frequency (RF):**

- **Description:** Wireless communication relies on radio frequency waves to transmit data between devices.
- **Key Points:** RF waves travel through the air and can be affected by interference, obstacles, and distance.

## Flash Card # 442

**Frequency Bands:**

- **Description:** Wireless signals operate within specific frequency bands allocated by regulatory bodies.

 

- **Key Points:** Common frequency bands include 2.4 GHz and 5 GHz for Wi-Fi, with each band having its advantages and limitations.

## Flash Card # 443

**Modulation:**

- **Description:** Modulation is the process of encoding digital data onto an analog carrier wave for transmission.
- **Key Points:** Different modulation techniques, such as amplitude modulation (AM) and frequency modulation (FM), are used to transmit data over wireless networks.

## Flash Card # 444

**Propagation:**

- **Description:** Propagation refers to how radio waves travel through different mediums, such as air, water, or obstacles.
- **Key Points:** Factors like reflection, diffraction, and absorption affect the propagation of radio waves, influencing signal strength and quality.

## Flash Card # 445

**Multipath Fading:**

- **Description:** Multipath fading occurs when radio waves take multiple paths to reach a receiver, leading to signal interference and distortion.
- **Key Points:** Techniques like diversity antennas and equalization are used to mitigate the effects of multipath fading in wireless communication.

 

## Flash Card # 446

**Line-of-Sight (LOS) vs. Non-Line-of-Sight (NLOS):**

- **Description:** LOS communication occurs when there is a direct, unobstructed path between transmitter and receiver, while NLOS communication involves obstacles or reflections.
- **Key Points:** LOS communication typically offers better signal strength and reliability compared to NLOS communication.

## Flash Card # 447

**Signal Strength and Signal-to-Noise Ratio (SNR):**

- **Description:** Signal strength measures the power of a wireless signal, while SNR compares the strength of the signal to background noise.
- **Key Points:** Higher signal strength and SNR values indicate better wireless performance and fewer transmission errors.

## Flash Card # 448

**Channel Bonding:**

- **Description:** Channel bonding combines multiple adjacent frequency channels to increase bandwidth and improve data transmission rates.
- **Key Points:** Channel bonding is commonly used in Wi-Fi networks to achieve higher throughput and reduce congestion.

 

### Flash Card # 449

**Interference:**

- **Description:** Interference occurs when unwanted signals disrupt wireless communication, leading to decreased performance and reliability.
- **Key Points:** Interference sources include other wireless devices, electronic appliances, and environmental factors like weather conditions.

### Flash Card # 450

**Security:**

- **Description:** Wireless networks require security measures to protect data from unauthorized access and eavesdropping.
- **Key Points:** Techniques like encryption, authentication, and access control are used to secure wireless communication and prevent security breaches.

### Flash Card # 451

**Antenna Diversity:**

- **Description:** Antenna diversity involves using multiple antennas to improve signal reliability and coverage.
- **Key Points:** Diversity techniques such as spatial diversity and polarization diversity help mitigate signal fading and improve overall wireless performance.

 

## Flash Card # 452

**Beamforming:**

- **Description:** Beamforming is a technique used to focus wireless signals in specific directions, improving signal strength and coverage.
- **Key Points:** Beamforming can be implemented using phased array antennas or adaptive antenna arrays to enhance signal reception and transmission.

## Flash Card # 453

**Channel Capacity:**

- **Description:** Channel capacity refers to the maximum data rate that can be transmitted over a wireless channel.
- **Key Points:** Factors affecting channel capacity include bandwidth, modulation scheme, and signal-to-noise ratio (SNR), with higher capacity channels supporting faster data rates.

## Flash Card # 454

**Propagation Delay:**

- **Description:** Propagation delay is the time it takes for a signal to travel from transmitter to receiver.
- **Key Points:** Propagation delay depends on the distance between devices and the speed of light, influencing the latency of wireless communication links.

 

## Flash Card # 455

**Wireless Standards and Protocols:**

- **Description:** Wireless standards define the specifications and protocols for wireless communication technologies.
- **Key Points:** Common wireless standards include IEEE 802.11 (Wi-Fi), Bluetooth, Zigbee, and cellular standards like LTE and 5G.

## Flash Card # 456

**Interference Mitigation Techniques:**

- **Description:** Interference mitigation techniques are used to minimize the impact of interference on wireless communication.
- **Key Points:** Techniques include frequency hopping, dynamic frequency selection (DFS), and interference avoidance mechanisms to maintain signal quality in the presence of interference sources.

## Flash Card # 457

**Wireless Access Points (APs):**

- **Description:** Wireless access points are devices that enable wireless devices to connect to a wired network.
- **Key Points:** APs provide Wi-Fi coverage and manage wireless connections, supporting multiple clients and providing network authentication and encryption.

 

### Flash Card # 458

**Channel Utilization:**

- **Description:** Channel utilization measures the efficiency of wireless channels in carrying data traffic.
- **Key Points:** High channel utilization indicates heavy network traffic and potential congestion, while low utilization may indicate underutilization of available resources.

### Flash Card # 459

**Roaming:**

- **Description:** Roaming allows wireless devices to maintain connectivity while moving between different access points or network areas.
- **Key Points:** Seamless roaming relies on protocols like IEEE 802.11r (Fast BSS Transition) and IEEE 802.11k (Radio Resource Measurement) to optimize handover and maintain connectivity during mobility.

### Flash Card # 460

**Wireless Site Surveys:**

- **Description:** Wireless site surveys assess the wireless environment to optimize network coverage, performance, and reliability.
- **Key Points:** Site surveys involve analyzing signal strength, interference levels, and environmental factors to design and deploy wireless networks effectively.

 

## Flash Card # 461

**Propagation Models:**

- **Description:** Propagation models describe how wireless signals propagate through different environments.
- **Key Points:** Common propagation models include free space, two-ray ground, and log-distance path loss models, used to estimate signal strength and coverage in various scenarios.

## Flash Card # 462

**Mesh Networking:**

- **Description:** Mesh networking is a decentralized network topology where nodes relay data for each other, enhancing coverage and resilience.
- **Key Points:** Mesh networks are self-configuring and self-healing, making them suitable for dynamic and challenging environments like smart cities and industrial IoT deployments.

## Flash Card # 463

**Wireless Security Threats:**

- **Description:** Wireless networks face security threats such as eavesdropping, unauthorized access, and denial-of-service (DoS) attacks.
- **Key Points:** Security measures like WPA2/WPA3 encryption, strong authentication, and intrusion detection systems (IDS) are essential to mitigate wireless security risks.

 

## Flash Card # 464

**Channel Interference Types:**

- **Description:** Channel interference can be caused by co-channel interference, adjacent channel interference, and non-802.11 interference sources.
- **Key Points:** Co-channel interference occurs when devices share the same frequency channel, while adjacent channel interference occurs when devices operate on nearby channels, leading to signal degradation.

## Flash Card # 465

**Propagation Characteristics:**

- **Description:** Propagation characteristics describe how wireless signals behave in different environments, such as indoor, outdoor, and urban settings.
- **Key Points:** Factors like reflection, diffraction, and scattering affect signal propagation, influencing coverage area and signal quality.

## Flash Card # 466

**Dynamic Frequency Selection (DFS):**

- **Description:** DFS is a mechanism that allows Wi-Fi devices to detect and avoid interference from radar systems operating in the same frequency band.
- **Key Points:** DFS is required for Wi-Fi devices operating in certain frequency bands (e.g., 5 GHz) to comply with regulatory requirements and ensure interference-free operation.

 

## Flash Card # 467

**Wireless Coexistence:**

- **Description:** Wireless coexistence refers to the ability of different wireless technologies to operate together in the same environment without interfering with each other.
- **Key Points:** Techniques like coexistence protocols, spectrum sharing, and interference mitigation mechanisms enable multiple wireless technologies to coexist harmoniously.

## Flash Card # 468

**Wireless LAN Controllers (WLCs):**

- **Description:** Wireless LAN controllers are centralized devices that manage and control multiple access points in a wireless network.
- **Key Points:** WLCs provide features like centralized management, security policy enforcement, and mobility support, enhancing the scalability and manageability of wireless deployments.

## Flash Card # 469

**Channel Bonding vs. Channel Width:**

- **Description:** Channel bonding combines multiple adjacent frequency channels to increase bandwidth, while channel width refers to the size of a single frequency channel.
- **Key Points:** Channel bonding increases throughput by using wider frequency bands, but may lead to increased interference and reduced spectrum availability for neighboring devices.

 

## Flash Card # 470

**Dynamic Frequency Hopping:**

- **Description:** Dynamic frequency hopping is a technique used in wireless communication to switch between different frequency channels to avoid interference and improve reliability.
- **Key Points:** Dynamic frequency hopping is commonly used in Bluetooth and other wireless technologies to maintain connectivity in noisy and congested environments.

## Flash Card # 471

**Wireless Spectrum Allocation:**

- **Description:** Wireless spectrum allocation refers to the process of assigning frequency bands to different wireless technologies and services.
- **Key Points:** Regulatory bodies allocate spectrum to ensure coexistence between different wireless technologies and minimize interference.

## Flash Card # 472

**Wireless LAN Architecture:**

- **Description:** Wireless LAN architecture defines the structure and components of a wireless network, including access points, controllers, and client devices.
- **Key Points:** WLAN architectures can be centralized (controller-based) or distributed (controller-less), each offering unique advantages and trade-offs in terms of scalability, management, and performance.

 

### Flash Card # 473

**Wireless Signal Propagation Models:**

- **Description:** Signal propagation models describe how wireless signals propagate through various environments, such as free space, indoor, and outdoor environments.
- **Key Points:** Common propagation models include the Friis transmission equation, log-distance path loss model, and Okumura-Hata model, used to predict signal coverage and strength in different scenarios.

### Flash Card # 474

**Wireless Interference Sources:**

- **Description:** Wireless interference can be caused by external sources like microwave ovens, Bluetooth devices, and neighboring networks operating on the same frequency band.
- **Key Points:** Interference mitigation techniques such as frequency hopping, adaptive channel selection, and interference detection algorithms help minimize the impact of interference on wireless communication.

### Flash Card # 475

**Wireless Access Control Methods:**

- **Description:** Wireless access control methods regulate access to wireless networks and resources, ensuring security and compliance with network policies.
- **Key Points:** Access control methods include MAC address filtering, WPA/WPA2/WPA3 authentication, IEEE 802.1X/EAP authentication, and captive portal authentication, each offering varying levels of security and flexibility.

 

## Flash Card # 476

**Wireless LAN Roaming Protocols:**

- **Description:** Roaming protocols enable seamless handover of wireless clients between different access points within the same network, ensuring uninterrupted connectivity.
- **Key Points:** Roaming protocols such as IEEE 802.11r (Fast BSS Transition), IEEE 802.11k (Radio Resource Measurement), and IEEE 802.11v (Wireless Network Management) optimize roaming performance and reduce latency during handover.

## Flash Card # 477

**Wireless Site Survey Techniques:**

- **Description:** Wireless site surveys assess RF coverage, signal strength, and interference levels to optimize the design and deployment of wireless networks.
- **Key Points:** Site survey techniques include passive and active surveys, predictive modeling, and spectrum analysis, helping identify coverage gaps, interference sources, and optimal AP placement.

## Flash Card # 478

**Wireless Mesh Networking:**

- **Description:** Wireless mesh networking is a decentralized architecture where nodes communicate with each other to relay data, forming a self-healing and resilient network.
- **Key Points:** Mesh networking is used in applications like smart cities, industrial IoT, and outdoor deployments where traditional infrastructure is impractical or cost-prohibitive.

 

## Flash Card # 479

**Wireless Security Best Practices:**

- **Description:** Wireless security best practices include implementing strong encryption, enabling secure authentication methods, regularly updating firmware, and segmenting wireless traffic from wired networks.
- **Key Points:** Robust security measures are essential to protect wireless networks from unauthorized access, data breaches, and cyberattacks.

## Flash Card # 480

**Wireless QoS (Quality of Service):**

- **Description:** Wireless QoS mechanisms prioritize and manage network traffic to ensure optimal performance for critical applications and services.
- **Key Points:** QoS techniques such as Wi-Fi Multimedia (WMM), traffic shaping, and admission control help minimize latency, jitter, and packet loss in wireless networks, improving user experience and application performance.

## Flash Card # 481

**Term:** Virtualization

**Function:** Creates virtual versions of computer resources like servers, storage, and networks. These virtual resources can be used and managed independently from the underlying physical hardware.

## Flash Card # 482

**Benefits of Virtualization:**

- **Improved server utilization:** Run multiple virtual servers on a single physical server, maximizing hardware resources.
- **Increased agility:** Quickly provision and deploy new virtual machines for faster application development and testing.
- **Cost savings:** Reduce hardware costs by consolidating multiple physical servers onto fewer machines.
- **Improved disaster recovery:** Easily migrate virtual machines between physical servers for better disaster recovery and business continuity.

## Flash Card # 483

**Types of Virtualization:**

- **Server virtualization:** Creates virtual machines (VMs) that emulate physical servers with their own operating systems and applications.
- **Container virtualization:** Packages applications with their dependencies into lightweight, portable containers that share the underlying operating system of the host machine.
- **Network virtualization:** Creates virtual networks that can be isolated from the physical network infrastructure, providing flexibility and security.

## Flash Card # 484

**Server Virtualization:**

- Uses a hypervisor software layer that sits between the physical hardware and the virtual machines.
- The hypervisor manages the allocation of resources (CPU, memory, storage) to each VM and ensures they run independently.

 

- Popular hypervisors include VMware ESXi, Microsoft Hyper-V, and KVM.

**Flash Card # 485**

**Containers:**

- More lightweight and portable than VMs.
- Share the host operating system kernel, reducing resource overhead compared to VMs.
- Ideal for deploying microservices and cloud-native applications.
- Popular container platforms include Docker and Kubernetes.

**Flash Card # 486**

**VRFs (Virtual Routing and Forwarding):**

- Enables the creation of multiple virtual routing instances within a single physical router.
- Each VRF has its own routing table and forwarding rules, allowing for network segmentation and isolation.
- Useful for creating secure and independent virtual networks on a single physical infrastructure.

**Flash Card # 487**

**Choosing the Right Virtualization Technology:**

- **Server virtualization:** Suitable for traditional applications requiring dedicated operating systems.
- **Containers:** Ideal for microservices and cloud-native deployments where resource efficiency and portability are critical.

 

- **VRFs:** Useful for creating isolated network segments within a single physical network.

**Flash Card # 488**

**Security Considerations in Virtualization:**

- Secure the hypervisor and container platform to prevent unauthorized access.
- Implement proper access controls for virtual resources.
- Monitor virtual environments for suspicious activity.

**Flash Card # 489**

**The Future of Virtualization:**

- Continued development of container technologies and container orchestration platforms.
- Integration of virtualization with cloud computing and Software-Defined Networking (SDN) for more dynamic and automated infrastructure management.
- Increased focus on security considerations in virtualized environments.

**Flash Card # 490**

**Benefits of Understanding Virtualization Fundamentals:**

- Enables efficient IT resource utilization and management.
- Provides flexibility and agility for deploying and scaling applications.
- Improves disaster recovery capabilities and business continuity.
- Enhances network security through network segmentation.

 

- A valuable skill for IT professionals in today's cloud-centric world.

## Flash Card # 491

**Term:** Hypervisor Types

- **Type 1 Hypervisor (Bare-metal):** Installed directly on the physical hardware, providing direct access to resources. Offers higher performance but requires dedicated hardware. (e.g., VMware ESXi, Microsoft Hyper-V)
- **Type 2 Hypervisor (Hosted):** Runs on top of an existing operating system, offering flexibility for running VMs on desktops or laptops. Lower performance compared to bare-metal hypervisors. (e.g., VirtualBox, VMware Workstation)

## Flash Card # 492

**Virtual Machine Management:**

- Tools like vCenter Server (VMware) or System Center Virtual Machine Manager (Microsoft) provide centralized management for provisioning, deploying, monitoring, and migrating virtual machines.
- Automation tools can be used to streamline VM lifecycle management tasks.

## Flash Card # 493

**Container Orchestration:**

- Container platforms like Docker require orchestration tools like Kubernetes for managing the deployment, scaling, and networking of containerized applications.

 

- Kubernetes provides features like service discovery, load balancing, and health checks for containerized workloads.

**Flash Card # 494**

**Storage Virtualization:**

- Creates a layer of abstraction between physical storage devices and the servers that access them.
- Enables features like storage pooling, thin provisioning, and replication for improved storage efficiency and data protection.
- Popular storage virtualization solutions include SAN (Storage Area Network) and NAS (Network Attached Storage).

**Flash Card # 495**

**Network Virtualization Technologies:**

- **VLANs (Virtual LANs):** Logically segment a physical network into multiple broadcast domains, improving security and network management.
- **VXLAN (Virtual Extensible LAN):** Enables overlay networks that can be stretched across physical networks, useful for data center environments.
- **SDN (Software-Defined Networking):** Decouples the data plane (packet forwarding) from the control plane (network programming), allowing for more flexible and programmable network management.

**Flash Card # 496**

**Virtual Machine Live Migration:**

 

- Ability to migrate running virtual machines between physical servers without downtime.
- Requires shared storage and compatible hypervisors for seamless migration.
- Improves server utilization and enables planned hardware maintenance without service interruptions.

## Flash Card # 497

**Security Considerations for Containers:**

- Container images can contain vulnerabilities. Implement vulnerability scanning and patching for container images.
- Secure container registries to prevent unauthorized access to container images.
- Enforce proper network isolation between containers using container networking policies.

## Flash Card # 498

**Benefits of Virtualization in Cloud Computing:**

- Enables on-demand provisioning of virtual resources like servers, storage, and networking.
- Improves scalability and elasticity for cloud applications.
- Facilitates multi-tenancy, allowing multiple users to share physical infrastructure securely.

## Flash Card # 499

**Virtual Desktop Infrastructure (VDI):**

- Provides virtual desktops to users, accessed remotely from any device.

 

- Improves desktop management and security, offering centralized control over user desktops.
- Requires powerful server infrastructure and appropriate network bandwidth for optimal performance.

## Flash Card # 500

**The Future of Virtualization: Hyperconverged Infrastructure (HCI):**

- Integrates compute, storage, and networking resources into a single, pre-configured system.
- Offers simplified deployment, management, and scalability for virtualized environments.
- Gaining popularity due to its ease of use and scalability for edge computing and smaller IT environments.

## Flash Card # 501

**Term:** Resource Management in Virtualization

- Efficient resource allocation (CPU, memory, storage) is crucial for optimal performance of virtual machines and containers.
- Hypervisors and container platforms offer resource management features like quotas, shares, and reservations to prioritize resource allocation.

## Flash Card # 502

**Monitoring Virtualization Performance:**

- Tools like vCenter Server (VMware) or System Center Virtual Machine Manager (Microsoft) provide performance metrics for CPU, memory, storage, and network utilization in virtual environments.

 

- Monitor resource utilization to identify bottlenecks and optimize VM or container placement.

**Flash Card # 503**

**Virtual Machine Sprawl:**

- Uncontrolled creation of virtual machines can lead to resource waste and management complexity.
- Implement VM lifecycle management processes to prevent sprawl and optimize resource utilization.
- Regularly review and decommission unused or underutilized VMs.

**Flash Card # 504**

**Live Migration Best Practices:**

- Ensure sufficient shared storage bandwidth and network connectivity for smooth live migration.
- Consider VM workload (CPU, memory intensity) when planning migrations to minimize performance impact.
- Test live migration procedures in a non-production environment before performing them in production.

**Flash Card # 505**

**Troubleshooting Virtual Machine Issues:**

- Analyze resource utilization metrics to identify resource bottlenecks causing performance problems for VMs.
- Check VM logs for error messages or warnings that might indicate issues with the operating system or applications running within the VM.

 

- Utilize hypervisor tools for troubleshooting VM connectivity or network configuration problems.

**Flash Card # 506**

**Container Orchestration Troubleshooting:**

- Kubernetes provides logs and monitoring tools for troubleshooting container deployments and failures.
- Analyze container logs to identify application errors or resource limitations.
- Use Kubernetes troubleshooting tools to diagnose network connectivity issues between containers or with external services.

**Flash Card # 507**

**Storage Virtualization Troubleshooting:**

- Monitor storage performance metrics like IOPS (Input/output Operations Per Second) and latency to identify storage bottlenecks.
- Analyze storage logs for errors related to disk failures or performance issues.
- Consider storage replication and failover mechanisms to ensure data availability during storage hardware failures.

**Flash Card # 508**

**Network Virtualization Troubleshooting:**

- Utilize network monitoring tools to diagnose connectivity issues within virtual networks.
- Verify network segmentation rules and firewall configurations to ensure proper traffic flow between virtual resources.

 

- In SDN environments, analyze SDN controller logs for configuration errors or network pathing problems.

**Flash Card # 509**

**Security Considerations in Troubleshooting:**

- Maintain security best practices even during troubleshooting activities.
- Avoid granting excessive permissions for troubleshooting purposes.
- Document troubleshooting steps and findings for future reference and knowledge sharing.

**Flash Card # 510**

**Importance of Continuous Learning:**

- Virtualization technologies are constantly evolving. Stay updated with new features, best practices, and troubleshooting techniques for different virtualization platforms.
- Online resources, communities, and vendor certifications can be valuable resources for ongoing learning and development in the virtualization field.

**Flash Card # 511**

**Term:** Cost Optimization in Virtualization

- Virtualization can optimize resource utilization and reduce hardware costs, but proper management is key.
- Right-sizing virtual machines by allocating appropriate CPU, memory, and storage resources can prevent resource waste.

 

- Utilize tools for VM placement optimization to balance resource utilization across physical servers.

**Flash Card # 512**
**Cloud Cost Optimization:**

- Cloud providers offer various pricing models for virtual resources (on-demand, reserved instances, spot instances).
- Choose the right pricing model based on workload requirements and cost considerations.
- Utilize cloud cost management tools provided by cloud platforms to identify and optimize cloud spending.

**Flash Card # 513**
**Serverless Computing:**

- A cloud computing model where server management is entirely handled by the cloud provider.
- Pay only for the resources consumed by your application during execution.
- Ideal for event-driven workloads or applications with unpredictable usage patterns.

**Flash Card # 514**
**Impact of Serverless on Virtualization:**

- Serverless computing can potentially reduce reliance on traditional virtual machines for certain workloads.
- However, virtual machines will still be essential for applications requiring more control or specific operating system environments.

 

## Flash Card # 515

**Microservices Architecture and Virtualization:**

- Microservices architecture breaks down applications into smaller, independent services.
- Containers are often used to deploy microservices due to their portability and scalability.
- Virtual machines can still be used for larger services or those requiring specific operating systems.

## Flash Card # 516

**Virtualization and Artificial Intelligence (AI):**

- AI can be used to automate resource management tasks in virtual environments, optimizing resource allocation and performance.
- Machine learning can be used for predictive maintenance of virtual infrastructure components.

## Flash Card # 517

**The Rise of Multi-Cloud and Hybrid Cloud Deployments:**

- Organizations may use a combination of public cloud, private cloud, and on-premises infrastructure.
- Virtualization technologies can facilitate workload portability across different cloud environments.
- Management tools are evolving to support multi-cloud and hybrid cloud deployments.

 

## Flash Card # 518

**Virtual Reality (VR) and Virtualization:**

- VR applications can be resource-intensive. Virtualization technologies can help optimize resource allocation for VR workloads.
- Cloud-based VR solutions leverage virtualization for scalability and remote access to VR experiences.

## Flash Card # 519

**The Future of Virtualization: Automation and Orchestration:**

- Increased use of automation and orchestration tools for provisioning, managing, and scaling virtualized resources.
- Integration with cloud platforms and DevOps methodologies for continuous delivery and lifecycle management of virtualized applications.

## Flash Card # 520

**The Evolving Role of IT Professionals:**

- Virtualization skills will remain essential, but the focus will shift towards automation, orchestration, and managing complex hybrid and multi-cloud environments.
- Continuous learning and adaptation will be crucial for IT professionals to succeed in the evolving world of virtualization.

 

### Flash Card # 521

**Switch:**

- **Description:** A switch is a network device that connects devices within a local area network (LAN) and forwards data based on MAC addresses.
- **Key Points:** Switches operate at Layer 2 (Data Link Layer) of the OSI model and use MAC address tables to make forwarding decisions.

### Flash Card # 522

**MAC Address:**

- **Description:** A Media Access Control (MAC) address is a unique identifier assigned to network interfaces for communication within a network.
- **Key Points:** MAC addresses are typically expressed as hexadecimal values and are used by switches to identify devices connected to the network.

### Flash Card # 523

**Port:**

- **Description:** A port on a switch is a physical or virtual connection point used to connect network devices, such as computers, printers, and servers.
- **Key Points:** Each port on a switch represents a separate collision domain and may be configured with specific settings and features.

 

### Flash Card # 524

**VLAN (Virtual Local Area Network):**

- **Description:** A VLAN is a logical segmentation of a network that allows devices to be grouped together based on criteria such as department, function, or location.
- **Key Points:** VLANs enable network administrators to isolate traffic, improve network performance, and enhance security by controlling communication between devices.

### Flash Card # 525

**Trunk:**

- **Description:** A trunk is a network link that carries traffic for multiple VLANs, allowing VLAN information to be transmitted between switches.
- **Key Points:** Trunk links use tagging mechanisms such as IEEE 802.1Q or ISL to differentiate between VLAN traffic and ensure proper VLAN assignment.

### Flash Card # 526

**Broadcast Domain:**

- **Description:** A broadcast domain is a logical division of a network where broadcast packets are forwarded to all devices within the domain.
- **Key Points:** Switches create separate broadcast domains for each VLAN, reducing the scope of broadcast traffic and improving network efficiency.

 

## Flash Card # 527

**Collision Domain:**

- **Description:** A collision domain is a segment of a network where collisions can occur between data packets transmitted by multiple devices.
- **Key Points:** Switches create separate collision domains for each port, reducing the likelihood of collisions and improving network performance compared to hubs.

## Flash Card # 528

**CAM Table (Content Addressable Memory Table):**

- **Description:** The CAM table is a hardware table in a switch that maps MAC addresses to port numbers.
- **Key Points:** The CAM table is used by switches to make forwarding decisions, enabling efficient data transmission within the network.

## Flash Card # 529

**STP (Spanning Tree Protocol):**

- **Description:** STP is a network protocol that prevents loops in Ethernet networks by blocking redundant paths and dynamically selecting the best path.
- **Key Points:** STP ensures network reliability and prevents broadcast storms by maintaining a loop-free topology in switched networks.

 

## Flash Card # 530

**Port Mirroring:**

- **Description:** Port mirroring is a feature that copies traffic from one port (or VLAN) to another port for analysis or monitoring purposes.
- **Key Points:** Port mirroring is commonly used for network troubleshooting, security monitoring, and traffic analysis in switched networks.

## Flash Card # 531

**VLANs (Virtual Local Area Networks):**

- **Description:** VLANs partition a single physical network into multiple logical networks, allowing for segmentation and isolation of traffic.
- **Key Points:** VLANs improve network security, performance, and management by separating broadcast domains and controlling traffic flow between devices.

## Flash Card # 532

**STP (Spanning Tree Protocol):**

- **Description:** STP prevents network loops in Ethernet networks by dynamically disabling redundant links and maintaining a loop-free topology.
- **Key Points:** STP elects a root bridge and calculates the shortest path to the root bridge, ensuring network resilience and redundancy while preventing broadcast storms.

 

### Flash Card # 533

**EtherChannel (Link Aggregation):**

- **Description:** EtherChannel bundles multiple physical links into a single logical link, increasing bandwidth and providing fault tolerance.
- **Key Points:** EtherChannel uses link aggregation protocols like LACP (Link Aggregation Control Protocol) or PAgP (Port Aggregation Protocol) to negotiate and manage link aggregation between switches.

### Flash Card # 534

**Port Security:**

- **Description:** Port security restricts access to switch ports based on MAC addresses, limiting the number of devices that can connect to a port.
- **Key Points:** Port security prevents unauthorized access and MAC address spoofing attacks by enforcing a maximum number of allowed MAC addresses per port and shutting down ports with unauthorized devices.

### Flash Card # 535

**IGMP Snooping (Internet Group Management Protocol Snooping):**

- **Description:** IGMP snooping monitors multicast traffic and dynamically forwards multicast packets only to the ports where multicast listeners are present.
- **Key Points:** IGMP snooping reduces multicast flooding, conserves network bandwidth, and improves multicast efficiency in Layer 2 switched networks.

 

## Flash Card # 536

**QoS (Quality of Service):**

- **Description:** QoS prioritizes network traffic based on defined policies, ensuring that critical applications receive preferential treatment over less important traffic.
- **Key Points:** QoS mechanisms such as traffic classification, queuing, and scheduling optimize network performance and meet service-level agreements (SLAs) for delay-sensitive applications like voice and video.

## Flash Card # 537

**Switchport Modes (Access, Trunk, and Hybrid):**

- **Description:** Switchport modes define how a switch port behaves and handles incoming traffic, including access, trunk, and hybrid modes.
- **Key Points:** Access ports carry traffic for a single VLAN, trunk ports carry traffic for multiple VLANs using VLAN tagging, and hybrid ports support both access and trunking functionalities.

## Flash Card # 538

**Port Mirroring (SPAN - Switched Port Analyzer):**

- **Description:** Port mirroring copies incoming and outgoing traffic on one switch port (the source port) to another port (the destination port) for network analysis and monitoring.
- **Key Points:** Port mirroring helps diagnose network issues, troubleshoot performance problems, and analyze network traffic patterns without disrupting normal network operation.

 

## Flash Card # 539

**Broadcast Domains:**

- **Description:** A broadcast domain is a logical division of a network where broadcast traffic is confined, typically bounded by routers or layer 3 devices.
- **Key Points:** Switches break broadcast domains, isolating broadcast traffic within individual VLANs to minimize network congestion and improve performance.

## Flash Card # 540

**Collision Domains:**

- **Description:** A collision domain is a segment of a network where collisions can occur between data packets, typically bounded by hubs or layer 1 devices.
- **Key Points:** Switches create separate collision domains for each port, reducing collisions and improving network efficiency compared to shared media environments like hubs.

## Flash Card # 541

**Switch Fabric:**

- **Description:** Switch fabric refers to the internal architecture of a switch that connects input and output ports, facilitating the forwarding of data between devices.
- **Key Points:** Switch fabric can be implemented using shared memory, shared bus, or crossbar architectures, depending on the switch's design and performance requirements.

 

## Flash Card # 542

**MAC Address Learning and Aging:**

- **Description:** Switches learn MAC addresses by inspecting source MAC addresses in incoming frames and associate them with the corresponding switch port in the MAC address table. Entries in the MAC address table age out over time if no frames are received from a particular MAC address.
- **Key Points:** MAC address learning and aging ensure efficient forwarding of frames within a switched network and prevent MAC address table overflow.

## Flash Card # 543

**Frame Switching:**

- **Description:** Frame switching is the process by which a switch forwards incoming frames to the appropriate destination port based on the destination MAC address.
- **Key Points:** Switches use the MAC address table to perform frame switching, forwarding frames directly to the destination port without flooding the entire network.

## Flash Card # 544

**Frame Flooding:**

- **Description:** Frame flooding occurs when a switch receives a frame with an unknown destination MAC address and forwards the frame to all ports except the source port.
- **Key Points:** Frame flooding is necessary to ensure that frames reach their intended destination when the MAC address is not in the switch's MAC address table, but it can lead to network congestion and inefficient use of bandwidth.

 

## Flash Card # 545

**MAC Address Table (CAM Table):**

- **Description:** The MAC address table (Content Addressable Memory table) stores MAC address-to-port mappings learned by the switch through frame forwarding.
- **Key Points:** The MAC address table is used by the switch to make forwarding decisions, ensuring that frames are forwarded only to the appropriate destination ports based on MAC addresses.

## Flash Card # 546

**Port Security Violation Modes:**

- **Description:** Port security violation modes determine the action taken by the switch when a security violation occurs, such as shutting down the port, sending an alert, or simply discarding the violating frames.
- **Key Points:** Port security violation modes include Shutdown, Protect, and Restrict, each providing different levels of security enforcement and mitigation of security threats.

## Flash Card # 547

**Loop Prevention Mechanisms:**

- **Description:** Loop prevention mechanisms such as Spanning Tree Protocol (STP) and Rapid Spanning Tree Protocol (RSTP) prevent the formation of network loops, which can cause broadcast storms and network instability.
- **Key Points:** These protocols dynamically disable redundant links in the network topology to maintain a loop-free topology and ensure network resilience.

 

## Flash Card # 548

**Frame Forwarding Methods:**

- **Description:** Frame forwarding methods determine how switches forward frames based on their destination MAC addresses, including store-and-forward, cut-through, and fragment-free forwarding.
- **Key Points:** Each forwarding method has different trade-offs in terms of latency, error detection, and efficiency, depending on the switch's capabilities and configuration.

## Flash Card # 549

**Port Mirroring vs. SPAN:**

- **Description:** Port mirroring (sometimes called SPAN - Switched Port Analyzer) copies traffic from one port or VLAN and forwards it to another port for network analysis, monitoring, or troubleshooting purposes.
- **Key Points:** Port mirroring is commonly used for monitoring network traffic, analyzing performance, and detecting security threats without disrupting normal network operation.

## Flash Card # 550

**Switchport Modes:**

- **Description:** Switchport modes define the behavior and functionality of switch ports, including access mode, trunk mode, and dynamic auto mode.
- **Key Points:** Access mode is used to connect end devices and carries traffic for a single VLAN, while trunk mode allows the transport of multiple VLANs over a single link. Dynamic auto mode enables ports to negotiate their operational mode dynamically with neighboring devices.

 

### Flash Card # 551

**Port Aggregation (EtherChannel):**

- **Description:** Port aggregation, also known as EtherChannel or link aggregation, combines multiple physical links into a single logical link to increase bandwidth and provide redundancy.
- **Key Points:** Port aggregation enhances network performance and fault tolerance by distributing traffic across multiple links and providing failover capabilities in case of link failure.

### Flash Card # 552

**Virtual LAN (VLAN) Trunking Protocol (VTP):**

- **Description:** VTP is a Cisco proprietary protocol used to synchronize VLAN configurations across multiple switches in a network, simplifying VLAN management and configuration.
- **Key Points:** VTP allows switches to exchange VLAN information, including VLAN IDs, names, and parameters, reducing manual configuration and ensuring consistency across the network.

### Flash Card # 553

**Switchport Security Features:**

- **Description:** Switchport security features, such as port security, DHCP snooping, and IP source guard, protect switch ports and mitigate security threats, such as unauthorized access and DHCP-based attacks.
- **Key Points:** These features enforce security policies, control access to network resources, and prevent malicious activities by monitoring and filtering traffic at the switch port level.

 

## Flash Card # 554

**IGMP Snooping (Internet Group Management Protocol Snooping):**

- **Description:** IGMP snooping is a Layer 2 multicast optimization technique that listens to IGMP messages between hosts and multicast routers to forward multicast traffic only to ports with interested receivers.
- **Key Points:** IGMP snooping reduces multicast traffic flooding and conserves network bandwidth by intelligently forwarding multicast packets to specific ports where multicast subscribers are located.

## Flash Card # 555

**Broadcast Storm:**

- **Description:** A broadcast storm occurs when broadcast packets are continuously forwarded and flooded throughout the network, causing excessive network traffic and performance degradation.
- **Key Points:** Broadcast storms can result in network congestion, packet loss, and service disruption, often caused by network loops or misconfigured devices.

## Flash Card # 556

**Port Channels:**

- **Description:** Port channels, also known as port-channel interfaces or EtherChannels, aggregate multiple physical links into a single logical link to increase bandwidth and provide link redundancy.
- **Key Points:** Port channels improve network performance and reliability by load balancing traffic across multiple links and providing failover capabilities in case of link failure.

 

## Flash Card # 557

**Trunking Protocols (802.1Q, ISL):**

- **Description:** Trunking protocols such as IEEE 802.1Q (dot1q) and Inter-Switch Link (ISL) encapsulate Ethernet frames with VLAN information for transmission over trunk links between switches.
- **Key Points:** Trunking protocols facilitate the transport of VLAN traffic across the network, allowing switches to maintain VLAN information and preserve VLAN boundaries.

## Flash Card # 558

**Loop Guard:**

- **Description:** Loop Guard is a Spanning Tree Protocol (STP) enhancement mechanism that prevents the formation of network loops by monitoring designated ports for unexpected changes in STP topology.
- **Key Points:** Loop Guard detects and blocks ports that transition from designated to alternate or blocking states, preventing network instability and potential packet loss.

## Flash Card # 559

**Root Bridge Election:**

- **Description:** Root Bridge Election is the process by which switches running Spanning Tree Protocol (STP) elect a root bridge to serve as the central point of the spanning tree topology.
- **Key Points:** The switch with the lowest Bridge ID (BID) is elected as the root bridge, with the BID composed of the Bridge Priority and MAC Address.

 

## Flash Card # 560

**STP Port States (Blocking, Listening, Learning, Forwarding):**

- **Description:** Spanning Tree Protocol (STP) defines four port states: Blocking, Listening, Learning, and Forwarding, to prevent network loops and ensure a loop-free topology.
- **Key Points:** Ports transition through these states during the STP convergence process, with each state serving a specific role in building and maintaining the spanning tree topology.

## Flash Card # 561

**BPDU (Bridge Protocol Data Unit):**

- **Description:** BPDU is a data unit used by Spanning Tree Protocol (STP) to exchange information between switches and maintain a loop-free topology.
- **Key Points:** BPDUs contain information such as Bridge ID, Port ID, and STP parameters, allowing switches to participate in the STP election process and negotiate the spanning tree topology.

## Flash Card # 562

**Rapid Spanning Tree Protocol (RSTP):**

- **Description:** Rapid Spanning Tree Protocol (RSTP) is an enhancement of the original Spanning Tree Protocol (STP) that reduces convergence time and provides faster network recovery in the event of topology changes.
- **Key Points:** RSTP achieves faster convergence by introducing new port roles (Discarding and Backup) and utilizing techniques such as PortFast, Edge Port, and Proposal/Agreement mechanisms.

 

## Flash Card # 563

**UDLD (UniDirectional Link Detection):**

- **Description:** UDLD is a Layer 2 protocol used to detect and prevent unidirectional links, where traffic can flow in only one direction, leading to connectivity issues and network instability.
- **Key Points:** UDLD monitors the physical connection between switches and detects unidirectional link failures, allowing affected ports to be placed into an error-disabled state to prevent traffic black-holing.

## Flash Card # 564

**Broadcast Storms:**

- **Description:** Broadcast storms occur when broadcast packets flood the network, consuming excessive bandwidth and degrading network performance.
- **Key Points:** Switches mitigate broadcast storms by filtering and forwarding broadcast packets only to the necessary ports, preventing them from being propagated throughout the entire network.

## Flash Card # 565

**Multicast Forwarding:**

- **Description:** Multicast forwarding enables the efficient transmission of multicast traffic to multiple recipients, conserving network bandwidth by sending a single copy of the data to multiple destinations.
- **Key Points:** Switches use multicast forwarding tables to manage multicast group membership and efficiently deliver multicast packets to interested receivers.

 

### Flash Card # 566

**Port Mirroring (SPAN):**

- **Description:** Port mirroring, also known as Switched Port Analyzer (SPAN), copies traffic from one switch port and forwards it to another port for analysis, monitoring, or troubleshooting purposes.
- **Key Points:** Port mirroring helps network administrators monitor traffic patterns, detect network anomalies, and troubleshoot performance issues without disrupting normal network operations.

### Flash Card # 567

**Switch Port Security:**

- **Description:** Switch port security features protect switch ports from unauthorized access and mitigate security threats by enforcing security policies, such as limiting the number of MAC addresses allowed per port or enabling port security violation actions.
- **Key Points:** Port security enhances network security by controlling access to network resources, preventing MAC address spoofing attacks, and detecting unauthorized devices connected to switch ports.

### Flash Card # 568

**Storm Control:**

- **Description:** Storm control prevents broadcast, multicast, or unknown unicast storms from overwhelming the network by monitoring and regulating the rate of incoming broadcast, multicast, or unknown unicast traffic.
- **Key Points:** Storm control thresholds can be configured to dynamically adjust the rate at which storm control actions, such as

 

dropping or throttling excess traffic, are triggered to protect the network from excessive broadcast or multicast traffic.

**Flash Card # 569**

**Loop Guard:**

- **Description:** Loop guard is a spanning tree protocol feature that prevents bridge protocol data units (BPDUs) from unexpected sources in the network, helping to maintain a loop-free topology and prevent network loops.
- **Key Points:** Loop guard monitors the consistency of BPDUs received on designated ports and places the port in loop-inconsistent state if expected BPDUs are not received, preventing network loops from forming.

**Flash Card # 570**

**BPDU Guard:**

- **Description:** BPDU guard is a spanning tree protocol feature that protects the network from misconfigured or unauthorized switches by disabling switch ports that receive BPDUs, which are typically not expected on end-user access ports.
- **Key Points:** BPDU guard helps prevent rogue switches or unauthorized network devices from disrupting the network by automatically disabling ports that receive unexpected BPDUs.

 

# Section - 2: Network Access

 

## Flash Card # 571

**VLAN Configuration:**

- **Definition:** VLANs are logical groupings of devices within a network, enabling segmentation for better management and security.
- **Configuration Modes:** VLANs can be configured in various modes such as access, trunk, or hybrid.
- **Access Ports:** Used to connect end devices to a specific VLAN.
- **Trunk Ports:** Used to carry traffic for multiple VLANs between switches.

## Flash Card # 572

**Trunking Protocols:**

- **IEEE 802.1Q:** Standard trunking protocol used to tag VLAN traffic on trunk links.
- **ISL (Inter-Switch Link):** Cisco proprietary trunking protocol, less commonly used compared to 802.1Q.
- **Dynamic Trunking Protocol (DTP):** Cisco protocol used to negotiate trunk links dynamically.

## Flash Card # 573

**VLAN Membership and Tagging:**

- **VLAN Membership:** Determines which VLAN a port belongs to.
- **Tagging:** Trunk ports tag Ethernet frames with VLAN information for identification.
- **Native VLAN:** Untagged VLAN on a trunk link, typically used for management traffic.

 

## Flash Card # 574

**VLAN Configuration Commands:**

- **vlan <VLAN_ID>:** Creates a VLAN with the specified VLAN ID.
- **name <VLAN_NAME>:** Assigns a name to the VLAN for easier identification.
- **switchport mode access:** Configures a port as an access port.
- **switchport mode trunk:** Configures a port as a trunk port.

## Flash Card # 575

**VLAN Verification Commands:**

- **show vlan brief:** Displays a brief summary of configured VLANs on a switch.
- **show interfaces <interface> switchport:** Provides information about the VLAN configuration of a specific interface.
- **show interfaces trunk:** Shows trunk port information, including allowed VLANs and encapsulation type.
- **show vlan id <VLAN_ID>:** Displays detailed information about a specific VLAN.

## Flash Card # 576

**InterVLAN Routing:**

- **Definition:** InterVLAN routing enables communication between devices in different VLANs.
- **Layer 3 Switches:** Can perform InterVLAN routing without the need for an external router.
- **Router Configuration:** Requires configuring subinterfaces or physical interfaces for each VLAN on the router.

 

## Flash Card # 577

**VLAN Best Practices:**

- **VLAN Segmentation:** Divide networks into VLANs based on logical groupings for better security and management.
- **Documentation:** Maintain accurate documentation of VLAN configurations for troubleshooting and future reference.
- **VLAN pruning:** Disable unnecessary VLANs on trunk links to optimize bandwidth and reduce unnecessary broadcast traffic.

## Flash Card # 578

**VTP (VLAN Trunking Protocol):**

- **Definition:** Cisco proprietary protocol used for managing VLAN configuration consistency across a network.
- **VTP Modes:** Server, Client, Transparent.
- **Configuration Revision Number:** Incremented each time a VLAN configuration change is made.
- **Caveats:** Misconfigurations or unintended actions in VTP can lead to VLAN inconsistencies or loss of connectivity.

## Flash Card # 579

**Extended VLAN Range:**

- **VLAN IDs:** Range from 1006 to 4094.
- **Usage:** Used for special purposes or in large-scale environments requiring more VLANs.
- **Compatibility:** Supported on certain Cisco switch models and software versions.

 

## Flash Card # 580

**VLAN Troubleshooting:**

- **Connectivity Issues:** Check VLAN configuration on the affected switch ports and trunk links.
- **VLAN Mismatch:** Verify that VLAN configurations match on both ends of trunk links.
- **Native VLAN Mismatch:** Ensure consistency of native VLAN settings on trunk links.
- **VTP Issues:** Verify VTP domain, mode, and revision number consistency.

## Flash Card # 581

**VLAN Security Features:**

- **Private VLANs (PVLANs):** Segment a single VLAN into multiple isolated sub-VLANs.
- **VLAN Access Control Lists (VACLs):** Filter traffic based on VLAN membership.
- **VLAN Hopping:** Protect against VLAN hopping attacks by disabling unused switch ports and enabling port security features.

## Flash Card # 582

**VLAN Design Considerations:**

- **Scalability:** Plan VLAN designs with future growth in mind to accommodate expanding network requirements.
- **Broadcast Domain Size:** Keep broadcast domains small to prevent excessive broadcast traffic.
- **Security Policies:** Align VLAN designs with security policies to enforce appropriate access controls and segmentation.
- **Performance:** Consider bandwidth requirements and traffic patterns when designing VLAN layouts.

 

## Flash Card # 583

**VLAN Migration Strategies:**

- **Incremental Migration:** Migrate VLANs gradually, one at a time, to minimize disruption.
- **Parallel Run:** Implement new VLANs alongside existing ones, then gradually transition devices to the new VLANs.
- **Verification:** Test VLAN configurations thoroughly before and after migration to ensure functionality and compliance with requirements.

## Flash Card # 584

**VLAN Pruning:**

- **Definition:** VLAN pruning is a technique used to restrict VLAN traffic from traversing trunk links where it's unnecessary.
- **Configuration:** Use the **switchport trunk allowed vlan <vlan-list>** command to specify which VLANs are allowed on a trunk link.
- **Benefits:** Reduces unnecessary broadcast and multicast traffic, improving overall network performance.
- **Considerations:** VLAN pruning should be used judiciously to avoid inadvertently blocking required VLAN traffic.

## Flash Card # 585

**VLAN Load Balancing:**

- **Definition:** VLAN load balancing distributes traffic across multiple physical links or switches to optimize bandwidth usage.
- **Configuration:** Implement EtherChannel or Link Aggregation Groups (LAGs) to bundle multiple physical links into a single logical link.
- **Benefits:** Improves network reliability, enhances performance, and provides redundancy.

 

- **Load-Balancing Algorithms:** Different load-balancing algorithms, such as source IP, destination IP, or MAC address, can be used to distribute traffic.

## Flash Card # 586

**VLAN Management Best Practices:**

- **Documentation:** Maintain up-to-date documentation of VLAN configurations, including VLAN IDs, names, and purposes.
- **Change Control:** Implement change control procedures to track and document any modifications to VLAN configurations.
- **Regular Audits:** Conduct regular audits of VLAN configurations to ensure compliance with organizational policies and security requirements.
- **Training:** Provide training to network administrators and staff on VLAN management best practices and procedures.

## Flash Card # 587

**VLAN Monitoring and Troubleshooting Tools:**

- **VLAN Membership Reports:** Use tools like SNMP-based network management systems to generate reports on VLAN membership and utilization.
- **VLAN Traceroute:** Troubleshoot inter-VLAN connectivity issues using tools that support VLAN-aware traceroute functionality.
- **Port Mirroring:** Set up port mirroring to capture and analyze VLAN traffic for troubleshooting and monitoring purposes.
- **Packet Capture:** Use packet capture tools like Wireshark to capture and analyze VLAN-tagged traffic for troubleshooting and analysis.

 

## Flash Card # 588

**VLAN Security Best Practices:**

- **VLAN Segmentation:** Segment the network into multiple VLANs based on functional requirements and security policies.
- **VLAN Access Control:** Implement VLAN access control lists (VACLs) or VLAN-based access control policies (VACPs) to control traffic between VLANs.
- **Port Security:** Enable port security features such as MAC address filtering and sticky MAC addresses to prevent unauthorized access to switch ports.
- **VLAN Encryption:** Implement VLAN encryption mechanisms to protect sensitive data transmitted between VLANs.

## Flash Card # 589

**VLAN Access Control Lists (VACLs):**

- **Definition:** VACLs are used to filter traffic within a VLAN based on specified criteria.
- **Configuration:** Apply VACLs to VLAN interfaces using the **vlan access-map** and **vlan filter** commands.
- **Filtering Criteria:** VACLs can filter traffic based on source or destination IP addresses, MAC addresses, protocols, or port numbers.
- **Use Cases:** VACLs are commonly used for security enforcement within VLANs, such as restricting access to specific resources or blocking certain types of traffic.

## Flash Card # 590

**Private VLANs (PVLANs):**

- **Definition:** PVLANs are used to segment a single VLAN into multiple isolated sub-VLANs.

 

- **Types:** Primary VLAN, Isolated VLAN, Community VLAN.
- **Configuration:** Configure PVLANs using the **switchport private-vlan** commands on supported switch platforms.
- **Use Cases:** PVLANs are often used in environments where strict isolation between devices within the same VLAN is required, such as in shared hosting environments or multi-tenant data centers.

## Flash Card # 591

**VLAN Configuration Distribution:**

- **Manual Configuration:** VLANs can be manually configured on each switch individually, which can be time-consuming and error-prone.
- **Dynamic VLAN Assignment:** Dynamic VLAN assignment protocols such as VMPS (VLAN Membership Policy Server) can automate VLAN assignment based on MAC address or user authentication.
- **VLAN Database Replication:** Some switches support VLAN database replication, allowing VLAN configurations to be automatically synchronized across multiple switches in a network.
- **Centralized Management:** Network management platforms can provide centralized management of VLAN configurations, simplifying the process of configuring and maintaining VLANs in large networks.

## Flash Card # 592

**VLAN Migration Strategies:**

- **Phased Migration:** Divide the network into phases and migrate VLANs gradually, starting with less critical VLANs and progressing to more critical ones.

 

- **Pilot Testing:** Conduct pilot tests of VLAN migrations in a controlled environment before deploying changes to the production network.
- **Rollback Plan:** Develop a rollback plan to revert to the previous VLAN configuration in case of any issues or unforeseen problems during the migration process.
- **Post-Migration Verification:** After migrating VLANs, verify that all network devices are properly configured and functioning as expected, and address any issues that arise.

## Flash Card # 593

**VLAN Tagging and Frame Format:**

- **VLAN Tagging:** Adds a 4-byte VLAN tag to Ethernet frames to identify the VLAN to which the frame belongs.
- **Frame Format:** The VLAN tag contains information such as the VLAN ID, priority, and EtherType.
- **IEEE 802.1Q:** Standard for VLAN tagging, which defines the format of the VLAN tag and the operation of VLAN trunking protocols.
- **VLAN Tag Stripping:** When a frame traverses a trunk link, the VLAN tag is removed before the frame is forwarded to the destination switch port.

## Flash Card # 594

What is the most common Ethernet trunking protocol used for interswitch connectivity?

802.1Q

 

**Flash Card # 595**

What command is used to configure a trunk on a Cisco switchport?
switchport mode trunk

**Flash Card # 596**

How can you verify if a trunk is formed between two switchports?
Use the show interface trunk command on either switch.

**Flash Card # 597**

What VLAN tagging method is used by 802.1Q trunking?
VLAN ID encapsulation

**Flash Card # 598**

What command can be used to verify CDP (Cisco Discovery Protocol) information on a switchport?
show cdp neighbors detail

**Flash Card # 599**

What information does CDP provide about neighboring devices?
Device type, device ID, port ID, and platform information.

 

## Flash Card # 600

What is a common troubleshooting step for verifying Layer 2 connectivity between switches?

Use a ping command between switch IP addresses or use tools like CDP to check for link and neighbor information.

## Flash Card # 601

What command can be used to verify basic Layer 3 connectivity between switches?

ping <switch_ip_address>

## Flash Card # 602

What static configuration is typically needed on switch interfaces for Layer 3 connectivity?

An IP address and subnet mask.

## Flash Card # 603

What are two key considerations when configuring trunk ports for interswitch connectivity?

- **Native VLAN:** Both trunks must be configured with the same native VLAN to allow untagged traffic.
- **Encapsulation mode:** Ensure both trunks use the same encapsulation mode (e.g., 802.1Q).

 

**Flash Card # 604**

How can you configure a switchport to be a trunk member for specific VLANs only?

Use the switchport trunk allowed vlan add <vlan_list> command to specify allowed VLANs.

**Flash Card # 605**

What troubleshooting steps can be taken if pings between switches fail?

- Verify physical connectivity (cables and port status).
- Check switchport configurations (mode, VLANs, trunking).
- Ensure IP addresses and subnet masks are correct on switch interfaces.
- Use tools like show interface and show ip route to diagnose further.

**Flash Card # 606**

What is VRRP (Virtual Router Redundancy Protocol) used for in interswitch connectivity?

VRRP provides fault tolerance by creating a virtual router with a single IP address that can failover between redundant switches.

**Flash Card # 607**

How can you verify the status of VRRP on a Cisco switch?

Use the show vrrp <VRRP group number> command to display information about the VRRP configuration and status.

 

## Flash Card # 608

What is the difference between trunk negotiation modes on Cisco switchports (on, desirable, auto)?

- **on:** Forces the port to be a trunk.
- **desirable:** Prefers trunking but can fall back to access mode if the neighbor doesn't support trunking.
- **auto:** Attempts to auto-negotiate trunking, falling back to access mode if negotiation fails.

## Flash Card # 609

What is STP (Spanning Tree Protocol) and how does it impact interswitch connectivity?

STP prevents loops in switched networks by electing a single path for data flow while blocking redundant paths. This can affect initial connectivity until the STP converges.

## Flash Card # 610

How can you configure link aggregation (LAG) for increased bandwidth between switches?

LAG combines multiple physical switchports into a single logical channel, increasing bandwidth and redundancy. Specific commands vary depending on the Cisco switch model.

## Flash Card # 611

What are some best practices for securing interswitch connectivity?

- Use VLANs to segment traffic and limit broadcast domains.

 

- Implement switchport security features like port security and AAA (Authentication, Authorization, and Accounting).
- Restrict access to switch management interfaces with strong passwords.

**Flash Card # 612**

What are some troubleshooting tools available for diagnosing complex interswitch connectivity issues?

- Use traceroute to identify the path packets take between switches and pinpoint potential hops with issues.
- Utilize debugging commands (with caution) to gain deeper insights into switch operation and packet flow.
- Leverage network monitoring tools to track switch performance and identify potential connectivity problems.

**Flash Card # 613**

What is the difference between Layer 2 and Layer 3 trunking?

- **Layer 2 Trunking:** Carries traffic for all VLANs across the trunk using VLAN tagging (e.g., 802.1Q).
- **Layer 3 Trunking:** Routes traffic between VLANs at Layer 3 (network layer), requiring separate IP interfaces on each switch for each VLAN carried on the trunk.

**Flash Card # 614**

What is MVRP (Multiple VLAN Registration Protocol) used for in interswitch connectivity?

 

MVRP dynamically registers VLANs on trunk ports, allowing switches to advertise and learn about the VLANs carried by neighboring switches.

**Flash Card # 615**

What are some considerations when configuring interswitch connectivity for Voice over IP (VoIP)?

- Prioritize VoIP traffic using QoS (Quality of Service) features on switchports.
- Consider using dedicated VLANs for VoIP traffic to isolate voice communication.
- Ensure low latency and minimal jitter on the interswitch links to maintain call quality.

**Flash Card # 616**

How can you configure a switchport for interswitch connectivity with a firewall?

- Depending on the firewall configuration, you might need to disable unused features like spanning-tree on the switchport connecting to the firewall.
- You may also need to configure static routes or access control lists (ACLs) to control traffic flow between the switch and the firewall.

**Flash Card # 617**

What are some emerging technologies impacting interswitch connectivity?

- **Software-Defined Networking (SDN):** Provides centralized control and programmability of network devices, including switch interconnectivity.

 

- **Converged Ethernet:** Combines data, voice, and video traffic on a single converged network infrastructure.

**Flash Card # 618**

You're troubleshooting connectivity between two switches. Pings between switch IP addresses fail. CDP shows the link is up. What's a likely cause?

Incorrect IP configuration on switch interfaces. Verify IP addresses and subnet masks are correct and interfaces are administratively up (no shutdown command).

**Flash Card # 619**

Devices on separate VLANs cannot communicate across switches. Both switches have trunks configured, but pings between devices fail. What could be wrong?

VLAN mismatch on the trunk ports. Ensure both trunks allow the specific VLANs the devices belong to (using switchport trunk allowed vlan add or similar).

**Flash Card # 620**

You suspect a loop is causing connectivity issues between switches. What information can help identify the loop?

Use the show spanning-tree command to view the STP topology and identify ports in blocking or looping states.

 

**Flash Card # 621**

Intermittent connectivity issues occur between switches. What troubleshooting steps can be taken?

- Check cable connections for loose wires or damage.
- Review switch logs for errors or warnings related to ports or trunking.
- Utilize tools like show interface to monitor interface counters for errors or dropped packets.

**Flash Card # 622**

After a switch configuration change, connectivity issues arise between switches. What's the best approach to troubleshoot?

- Isolate the change: Revert the configuration change and see if connectivity returns.
- Verify switch configurations: Double-check trunking settings, VLAN assignments, and any security features implemented.
- Utilize console access: Directly connect to the switch for troubleshooting commands if needed (with caution).

**Flash Card # 623**

**Layer 2 Discovery Protocols:**

- **Definition:** Layer 2 discovery protocols are used by networking devices to dynamically discover and advertise information about neighboring devices on the local network segment.
- **Purpose:** Facilitate network mapping, device identification, and troubleshooting by providing information such as device type, capabilities, and connectivity status.
- **Examples:** Cisco Discovery Protocol (CDP) and Link Layer Discovery Protocol (LLDP) are two common Layer 2 discovery protocols used in enterprise networks.

 

## Flash Card # 624

**Cisco Discovery Protocol (CDP):**

- **Definition:** CDP is a proprietary Layer 2 discovery protocol developed by Cisco Systems.
- **Functionality:** CDP allows Cisco devices to discover and share information about neighboring Cisco devices, including device type, IP address, and interface information.
- **Configuration:** CDP is enabled by default on Cisco devices, but can be globally enabled or disabled using the **cdp run or no cdp** run commands respectively.
- **Verification:** Use the **show cdp neighbors** command to display information about neighboring Cisco devices discovered via CDP.

## Flash Card # 625

**LLDP (Link Layer Discovery Protocol):**

- **Definition:** LLDP is an industry-standard Layer 2 discovery protocol defined in the IEEE 802.1AB standard.
- **Functionality:** LLDP allows networking devices from different vendors to exchange information about neighboring devices, such as system capabilities, device type, and port identifier.
- **Configuration:** LLDP is disabled by default on Cisco devices. It can be enabled globally using the **lldp run** command, and on specific interfaces using the **lldp transmit** and **lldp receive** commands.
- **Verification:** Use the **show lldp neighbors** command to display information about neighboring devices discovered via LLDP.

 

## Flash Card # 626

**CDP vs. LLDP:**

- **Vendor Support:** CDP is proprietary to Cisco devices, while LLDP is an industry-standard protocol supported by a wide range of networking vendors.
- **Configuration:** CDP is enabled by default on Cisco devices, whereas LLDP must be explicitly enabled if required.
- **Information Exchange:** CDP provides more detailed information about neighboring Cisco devices, while LLDP provides standardized information that can be exchanged between devices from different vendors.

## Flash Card # 627

**CDP and LLDP Configuration Verification:**

- Use the appropriate **show** commands to verify the configuration and operation of CDP and LLDP on Cisco devices.
- **For CDP:** Employ the **show cdp neighbors** command to display information about neighboring Cisco devices discovered via CDP.
- **For LLDP:** Utilize the **show lldp neighbors** command to view information about neighboring devices discovered via LLDP.

## Flash Card # 628

**CDP and LLDP Configuration Commands:**

- **CDP:** Use the **cdp run** command to globally enable CDP on a Cisco device. To disable CDP, employ the **no cdp run** command.
- **LLDP:** Utilize the **lldp run** command to globally enable LLDP on a Cisco device. Use the **lldp transmit** and **lldp receive** commands to configure LLDP transmission and reception on specific interfaces.

 

### Flash Card # 629

**Benefits of Layer 2 Discovery Protocols:**

- **Network Mapping:** Layer 2 discovery protocols facilitate the creation of accurate network maps by providing information about neighboring devices and their connections.
- **Troubleshooting:** These protocols aid in troubleshooting network connectivity issues by providing real-time information about neighboring devices and their status.
- **Automated Configuration:** Layer 2 discovery protocols can be used to automate network device provisioning and configuration tasks by dynamically discovering neighboring devices and their capabilities.

### Flash Card # 630

**CDP and LLDP Security Considerations:**

- **Disabling Discovery Protocols:** To enhance security, consider disabling CDP and LLDP on network devices where they are not required.
- **Access Control:** Restrict access to CDP and LLDP information by implementing appropriate access control measures, such as using access control lists (ACLs) or network segmentation.
- **Monitoring:** Regularly monitor CDP and LLDP traffic on the network to detect and mitigate any unauthorized or suspicious activity.

### Flash Card # 631

**Integration with Network Management Systems:**

- CDP and LLDP information can be integrated with network management systems (NMS) to provide comprehensive network monitoring and management capabilities.

 

- NMS platforms can utilize CDP and LLDP information to automatically discover and inventory network devices, track device connections, and monitor network topology changes.
- This integration enhances network visibility, simplifies device management, and improves overall network performance and reliability.

## Flash Card # 632

**Best Practices for Layer 2 Discovery Protocol Usage:**

- **Enable only as needed:** Enable CDP and LLDP only on interfaces where they are required for device discovery and network monitoring purposes.
- **Secure configurations:** Implement secure configurations for CDP and LLDP, including enabling authentication where supported and disabling unnecessary features.
- **Regular monitoring:** Regularly monitor CDP and LLDP traffic on the network to ensure proper operation and detect any anomalies or security threats.

## Flash Card # 633

**Cisco Discovery Protocol (CDP):**

- **Definition:** CDP is a proprietary Layer 2 protocol developed by Cisco for discovering and gathering information about directly connected Cisco devices.
- **Features:** Provides information about neighboring Cisco devices, including device type, IP address, platform, and port ID.
- **Configuration:** Enabled by default on Cisco devices, can be disabled globally or on specific interfaces using the **no cdp run or no cdp enable** commands.

 

- **Command:** Use **show cdp neighbors** to display information about neighboring Cisco devices discovered via CDP.

## Flash Card # 634

**LLDP (Link Layer Discovery Protocol):**

- **Definition:** LLDP is an industry-standard Layer 2 protocol used for network discovery and neighbor identification.
- **Standards:** Defined in IEEE 802.1AB and supported by a wide range of networking vendors.
- **Features:** Similar to CDP, provides information about neighboring devices, including device type, capabilities, and management addresses.
- **Configuration:** Enabled globally or on specific interfaces using the **lldp run or lldp enable** commands.
- **Command:** Use **show lldp neighbors** to display information about neighboring devices discovered via LLDP.

## Flash Card # 635

**CDP and LLDP Compatibility:**

- **Interoperability:** Cisco devices support both CDP and LLDP, allowing them to discover and exchange information with devices from other vendors.
- **Compatibility Mode:** Cisco devices can be configured to operate in CDP-only, LLDP-only, or mixed mode to support interoperability with devices using different discovery protocols.
- **Benefits:** Enabling both CDP and LLDP on Cisco devices enhances network visibility and facilitates interoperability in heterogeneous network environments.

 

## Flash Card # 636

**CDP and LLDP Timers:**

- **Advertisement Interval:** Determines how often CDP or LLDP advertisements are sent out by a device, typically configured in seconds.
- **Hold Time:** Specifies the amount of time a CDP or LLDP advertisement is considered valid before it expires, typically configured in seconds.
- **Default Values:** CDP advertisement interval is 60 seconds with a hold time of 180 seconds, while LLDP advertisement interval is typically 30 seconds with a hold time of 120 seconds.

## Flash Card # 637

**CDP and LLDP TLVs (Type-Length-Value):**

- **TLVs:** CDP and LLDP messages consist of TLVs, which contain specific information elements exchanged between devices.
- **Common TLVs:** Include device ID, port ID, capabilities, platform, software version, and management address TLVs.
- **Custom TLVs:** Additional TLVs can be defined for specific vendor extensions or proprietary information elements.

## Flash Card # 638

**CDP and LLDP Security Considerations:**

- **Information Exposure:** CDP and LLDP messages contain sensitive information about neighboring devices, which could be exploited by attackers.
- **Mitigation:** Disable CDP and LLDP on untrusted interfaces or enable features like CDP/LLDP authentication and encryption to protect against unauthorized access or tampering.

 

- **Best Practices:** Implement security policies to restrict the use of CDP and LLDP to trusted interfaces and monitor for unauthorized CDP/LLDP traffic on the network.

## Flash Card # 639

**CDP and LLDP Configuration Verification:**

- Use the **show cdp neighbors** or **show lldp neighbors** commands to verify neighboring devices discovered via CDP or LLDP.
- Verify CDP or LLDP configuration settings using the **show cdp or show lldp** commands to ensure that the protocols are enabled and configured correctly on the device.
- Use the **show cdp interfaces** or **show lldp interfaces** commands to view detailed information about CDP or LLDP on specific interfaces, including status and timers.

## Flash Card # 640

**CDP and LLDP Limitations:**

- **Layer 2 Only:** CDP and LLDP operate at Layer 2 and are limited to discovering directly connected neighbors within the same broadcast domain.
- **Limited Protocol Support:** While CDP is specific to Cisco devices, LLDP is an industry-standard protocol supported by various vendors but may lack certain Cisco-specific features.
- **Discovery Scope:** CDP and LLDP are primarily used for discovering neighboring devices and their attributes and may not provide comprehensive network visibility or topology information.

 

## Flash Card # 641

**CDP and LLDP Troubleshooting:**

- Use the **show cdp** or **show lldp** commands to verify the status and configuration of CDP or LLDP on the device.
- Check interface status and configuration using the **show interfaces** command to ensure that CDP or LLDP is enabled on the correct interfaces.
- Verify connectivity and Layer 2 reachability between devices by checking VLAN configurations, trunk links, and switchport settings.
- Analyze CDP or LLDP neighbor information to identify any inconsistencies or errors and troubleshoot accordingly.

## Flash Card # 642

**CDP and LLDP Configuration Best Practices:**

- Enable CDP or LLDP globally on all devices to facilitate network discovery and management.
- Configure CDP or LLDP on all relevant interfaces to ensure comprehensive visibility into the network topology.
- Regularly monitor and audit CDP or LLDP configurations and neighbor information to detect any anomalies or unauthorized devices.
- Implement security measures such as authentication, encryption, and access control to protect against CDP or LLDP-related security threats.

## Flash Card # 643

**CDP (Cisco Discovery Protocol):**

- Developed by Cisco Systems.

 

- Proprietary Layer 2 protocol.
- Provides information about Cisco devices directly connected to a switch.
- Enabled by default on Cisco devices.

**Flash Card # 644**

**LLDP (Link Layer Discovery Protocol):**

- Industry-standard Layer 2 protocol.
- Defined by IEEE 802.1AB.
- Provides similar functionality to CDP but is vendor-neutral.
- Supported by various networking vendors.

**Flash Card # 645**

**CDP and LLDP Information Elements:**

- **Device ID:** Name of the neighboring device.
- **Port ID:** Identifier of the neighboring device's port.
- **Capabilities:** Device's capabilities, such as whether it supports routing.
- **Platform:** Hardware platform of the neighboring device.

**Flash Card # 646**

**CDP and LLDP Configuration Commands:**

- **cdp run:** Globally enables CDP on a Cisco device.
- **lldp run:** Globally enables LLDP on a Cisco device.
- **cdp enable / no cdp enable**: Enables or disables CDP on a specific interface.

 

- **lldp transmit / no lldp transmit**: Enables or disables LLDP transmission on a specific interface.

**Flash Card # 647**

**CDP and LLDP Neighbor Information:**

- Use **show cdp neighbors** to display neighboring Cisco devices discovered via CDP.
- Use **show lldp neighbors** to display neighboring devices discovered via LLDP.
- Information includes device ID, port ID, capabilities, and platform.

**Flash Card # 648**

**CDP and LLDP Timers:**

- **Advertisement Interval:** How often CDP or LLDP messages are sent.
- **Hold Time:** How long CDP or LLDP information is considered valid.
- Default values vary between CDP and LLDP but can usually be adjusted.

**Flash Card # 649**

**CDP and LLDP Security Considerations:**

- **Information Leakage:** CDP and LLDP messages can reveal network topology information to potential attackers.
- **Disable on Untrusted Ports:** Turn off CDP and LLDP on ports that connect to untrusted networks or users.

 

- **Encryption and Authentication:** Implement features like CDP/LLDP authentication or encryption to secure protocol traffic.

**Flash Card # 650**

**CDP and LLDP Verification Commands:**

- Use **show cdp** to view CDP configuration and status information.
- Use **show lldp** to view LLDP configuration and status information.
- Additional commands provide detailed information about neighbors, timers, and interface settings.

**Flash Card # 651**

**CDP and LLDP Limitations:**

- **Limited to Layer 2:** CDP and LLDP operate only at Layer 2 and cannot provide information about devices beyond directly connected neighbors.
- **Interoperability Challenges:** Non-Cisco devices may not fully support CDP, while LLDP may lack certain features compared to CDP.
- **Limited Security:** CDP and LLDP do not provide strong security features, so additional measures may be needed to secure network devices.

**Flash Card # 652**

What is EtherChannel and what benefit does it provide?

EtherChannel bundles multiple physical Ethernet links into a single logical link, increasing bandwidth, redundancy, and fault tolerance.

 

**Flash Card # 653**

What protocol is commonly used for negotiating EtherChannels?

Link Aggregation Control Protocol (LACP) is used for automatic negotiation of EtherChannels between compatible devices.

**Flash Card # 654**

What are the configuration requirements for LACP EtherChannel on both switches?

- Identical channel-group number on both switches
- Same LACP mode (active or passive)
- Matching port speeds and duplex settings

**Flash Card # 655**

What commands are used to configure a Layer 2 EtherChannel on a Cisco switch?

- interface range port-channel <channel-number>
- channel-group <channel-number> mode active/passive (depending on desired mode)
- switchport mode trunk (on each member interface)

**Flash Card # 656**

What commands are used to verify a Layer 2 EtherChannel on a Cisco switch?

- show interface channel-group <channel-number> (displays channel status and member ports)
- show interfaces switchport mode trunk (on member interfaces)

 

## Flash Card # 657

How does Layer 3 EtherChannel differ from Layer 2 EtherChannel?

Layer 3 EtherChannel requires an IP address to be configured on the channel interface itself, allowing for routing between VLANs carried across the EtherChannel.

## Flash Card # 658

What additional configuration is needed for a Layer 3 EtherChannel?

- An IP address and subnet mask on the channel interface (interface port-channel <channel-number>)
- No switchport mode configuration needed on member interfaces (they operate at Layer 3)

## Flash Card # 659

How can you verify a Layer 3 EtherChannel on a Cisco switch?

- show interface channel-group <channel-number> (verify IP address and status)
- ping <channel_ip_address> (test connectivity using the channel interface IP)

## Flash Card # 660

What troubleshooting steps can be taken if an EtherChannel is not forming?

- Verify cable connections and switchport configurations on member interfaces.
- Ensure LACP mode and channel-group number match on both switches.

 

- Check switch logs for errors related to LACP or EtherChannel formation.

**Flash Card # 661**

What are some limitations of EtherChannel technology?

- Requires compatible switches that support LACP.
- Limited to a maximum of 8 member ports in a channel group (depending on switch model).
- Not all switch ports can be bundled into an EtherChannel.

**Flash Card # 662**

What are the different LACP modes (active, passive) and how do they impact channel formation?

- **Active:** Port actively negotiates with neighboring devices to form an EtherChannel.
- **Passive:** Port only responds to LACP messages from neighboring devices but doesn't initiate negotiation. (Use opposite modes on connected switches for them to agree on forming a channel).

**Flash Card # 663**

How can you configure a static EtherChannel (without LACP)?

While not recommended, static EtherChannel can be configured using `channel-group <channel-number> mode on` on each member interface. However, this bypasses negotiation and requires manual configuration on both switches.

 

**Flash Card # 664**

What is port channeling load balancing and how does it work with EtherChannel?

EtherChannel distributes traffic across member links using different algorithms like source MAC address or packet hashing. This helps balance load and utilize available bandwidth efficiently.

**Flash Card # 665**

How can you monitor the health and performance of an EtherChannel?

- Use show interface channel-group <channel-number> to view channel status, member ports, and traffic statistics.
- Utilize SNMP (Simple Network Management Protocol) to monitor EtherChannel performance metrics.

**Flash Card # 666**

What security considerations are important when using EtherChannel?

- Implement switch security features like port security and AAA to restrict unauthorized access on member interfaces.
- Be aware of potential security vulnerabilities associated with aggregation protocols like EtherChannel.

**Flash Card # 667**

What are some common troubleshooting steps for a failed member port in an EtherChannel?

- Verify the failing port is up and configured correctly (speed, duplex, etc.).
- Check cable connections for any loose wires or damage.

 

- Isolate the issue: Try disabling the failing port temporarily to see if the EtherChannel remains functional.
- Review switch logs for errors related to the specific member port.

**Flash Card # 668**

How can VLAN tagging be used with EtherChannel?

EtherChannel can carry traffic for multiple VLANs by using VLAN tagging (e.g., 802.1Q) on member ports. The switch configuration for the channel interface itself typically doesn't require any specific VLAN mode.

**Flash Card # 669**

What are some emerging technologies that might impact EtherChannel usage in the future?

- Multi-chassis Link Aggregation (MLAG): Enables link aggregation across multiple interconnected chassis devices, potentially replacing traditional EtherChannel in some scenarios.
- Converged Ethernet Fabrics: Offer high-bandwidth, low-latency fabrics for data center environments, potentially reducing reliance on point-to-point connections like EtherChannel.

**Flash Card # 670**

What best practices should be followed when configuring EtherChannel?

- Use dedicated switch ports for EtherChannel to avoid spanning-tree loops.
- Match cable lengths for member ports to ensure consistent signal timing.

 

- Document the EtherChannel configuration for future reference and troubleshooting.

**Flash Card # 671**

How can automation tools be used to manage EtherChannel configurations?
Network automation tools like Python scripts or configuration management platforms can be used to automate repetitive tasks like EtherChannel configuration across multiple switches, promoting consistency and reducing errors.

**Flash Card # 672**

What are some advanced LACP features that can be configured on Cisco switches?

- **LACP Key:** A unique identifier used for tie-breaking during channel formation when multiple paths are available.
- **Port Priority:** A value assigned to each port influencing its selection as a preferred link in the EtherChannel.
- **Minimum Links:** Setting a minimum number of ports required for the channel to be active (useful for ensuring redundancy).

**Flash Card # 673**

How can you troubleshoot a scenario where only some member ports participate in the EtherChannel?

- Verify port speed and duplex settings are consistent across all member interfaces.
- Ensure cable lengths are within recommended limits to avoid synchronization issues.

 

- Check for switch errors related to specific member ports that might be preventing them from joining the channel.

**Flash Card # 674**

What are some considerations when using EtherChannel with high availability protocols like HSRP (Hot Standby Router Protocol)?

- Ensure the HSRP virtual IP address is reachable via the EtherChannel interface for seamless failover.
- Consider using static routing on the channel interface to avoid potential routing issues during HSRP failover.

**Flash Card # 675**

How can QoS (Quality of Service) be implemented with EtherChannel?

QoS features on the switch can be used to prioritize traffic on specific member ports within the EtherChannel based on traffic types (e.g., voice, video).

**Flash Card # 676**

What are some security best practices when using EtherChannel with network access control (NAC) solutions?

- Configure NAC to enforce authentication and authorization on individual member ports within the EtherChannel, not just the channel interface itself.
- Consider using VLAN trunking with EtherChannel to further segment traffic and restrict unauthorized access based on VLAN membership.

 

### Flash Card # 677

You're troubleshooting a situation where an EtherChannel intermittently loses functionality. What could be causing this?

- **Faulty cable connections:** Check for loose wires or damaged cables on any member ports.
- **Port flapping:** Investigate switch logs for interface errors or flapping events on member ports.
- **Spanning-tree issues:** Verify STP convergence and ensure ports are not transitioning frequently (causing brief outages).

### Flash Card # 678

You suspect mismatched configurations might be causing EtherChannel problems. How can you diagnose this?

- Use show running-config on both switches to compare EtherChannel configurations (channel-group number, mode, member ports).
- Ensure switch software versions are compatible for proper LACP negotiation.

### Flash Card # 679

After adding a new switch to an existing EtherChannel, some devices connected to the new switch experience connectivity issues. What might be wrong?

- **Incorrect VLAN assignment:** Verify the new switch has the same VLANs configured on the ports that connect to the EtherChannel as the original switches.
- **Security restrictions:** Check for any firewall rules or port security settings on the new switch that might be blocking traffic.
- **Loop potential:** Ensure proper STP configuration on the new switch to avoid introducing loops when joining the EtherChannel.

 

## Flash Card # 680

How can advanced debugging tools be used to troubleshoot complex EtherChannel issues?

- Use debug lacp packets (with caution) to view LACP negotiation details and identify potential issues during channel formation.
- Leverage analyzer tools to capture traffic on member ports and analyze packet flow for errors or inconsistencies.

## Flash Card # 681

What are some best practices for documenting EtherChannel configurations?

- Document the channel-group number, member ports, and switch interfaces involved.
- Include LACP mode settings, any VLAN tagging configurations, and QoS settings applied to the EtherChannel.
- Note down the switch model and software versions for future reference.

## Flash Card # 682

**Rapid PVST+ Overview:**

- Rapid PVST+ is an extension of the original Spanning Tree Protocol (STP) developed by Cisco Systems.
- It provides rapid convergence and load balancing in networks with multiple VLANs.
- Rapid PVST+ operates on a per-VLAN basis, allowing for independent spanning tree instances for each VLAN.

 

### Flash Card # 683

**Bridge Protocol Data Units (BPDUs):**

- BPDUs are messages exchanged between switches to establish and maintain a loop-free topology.
- In Rapid PVST+, BPDUs carry information specific to each VLAN, including bridge priorities, port costs, and designated switch information.
- Rapid PVST+ BPDUs are transmitted and received on each VLAN, allowing for independent spanning tree calculations per VLAN.

### Flash Card # 684

**Rapid Convergence:**

- Rapid PVST+ enables faster convergence than traditional STP implementations.
- Convergence is achieved through mechanisms such as Rapid Spanning Tree Protocol (RSTP) and the use of port roles (e.g., designated, root, alternate, backup).
- Upon link failure or topology changes, Rapid PVST+ switches transition rapidly to new spanning tree states, reducing downtime and network instability.

### Flash Card # 685

**Port Roles in Rapid PVST+:**

- **Root Port:** Forwarding port towards the root bridge for each VLAN.
- **Designated Port:** Forwarding port selected on each segment to forward traffic towards the root bridge.
- **Alternate Port:** Backup port that is ready to transition to the designated role if the current designated port fails.
- **Backup Port:** Backup port that is ready to transition to the root port role if the current root port fails.

 

## Flash Card # 686

**Load Balancing:**

- Rapid PVST+ allows for load balancing across redundant links by actively using multiple spanning tree instances (one per VLAN).
- Load balancing is achieved by distributing VLAN traffic across different paths in the network.
- Each VLAN has its own spanning tree topology, enabling optimal forwarding paths for traffic in each VLAN independently.

## Flash Card # 687

**Root Bridge Election:**

- In Rapid PVST+, root bridge elections occur separately for each VLAN.
- The bridge with the lowest bridge ID (priority + MAC address) becomes the root bridge for the respective VLAN.
- Root bridge selection is crucial for determining the spanning tree topology and forwarding paths within each VLAN.

## Flash Card # 688

**Forwarding and Blocking States:**

- **Forwarding State:** Ports in this state are actively forwarding data frames.
- **Blocking State:** Ports in this state are in a listening and learning phase, but do not forward data frames.
- Rapid PVST+ switches transition rapidly between these states based on topology changes to ensure loop-free operation.

 

## Flash Card # 689

**Path Cost Calculation:**

- Path cost represents the cumulative cost of traversing links from a switch to the root bridge.
- Rapid PVST+ calculates path costs based on the speed (bandwidth) of the links.
- Lower path costs indicate preferred paths towards the root bridge and are used for determining the spanning tree topology.

## Flash Card # 690

**Topology Change Notification:**

- Rapid PVST+ rapidly detects changes in the network topology, such as link failures or topology changes.
- Upon detecting a topology change, switches immediately propagate notifications to other switches to recompute the spanning tree.
- This rapid notification process helps minimize the convergence time and ensures network stability in dynamic environments.

## Flash Card # 691

**Verification Commands:**

- Use **show spanning-tree vlan <vlan-id>** command to display the Rapid PVST+ spanning tree information for a specific VLAN.
- **show spanning-tree summary** provides a summary of the spanning tree instances configured on the switch.
- **show spanning-tree interface <interface>**displays the spanning tree status and port roles for a specific interface.
- **show spanning-tree root** shows the root bridge information for each VLAN.

 

## Flash Card # 692

**Bridge Priority:**

- Bridge Priority is a configurable value used in Rapid PVST+ to determine the root bridge.
- Lower Bridge Priority values are preferred; the default value is 32768.
- Bridge Priority combined with MAC address forms the Bridge ID, used in root bridge election.

## Flash Card # 693

**Root Port Election:**

- Root Port is the port on a non-root bridge with the lowest path cost to the root bridge.
- Path cost is determined by the cumulative cost of all links from the port to the root bridge.
- Rapid PVST+ selects the port with the lowest path cost as the Root Port for each VLAN.

## Flash Card # 694

**Designated Port Election:**

- Designated Port is the forwarding port selected on each LAN segment to forward traffic towards the root bridge.
- Rapid PVST+ selects the port with the lowest path cost to the root bridge as the Designated Port for each segment.
- Only one port per segment can be designated as the Designated Port.

 

### Flash Card # 695

**Alternate and Backup Ports:**

- Alternate Port is a backup port that is ready to become designated if the current Designated Port fails.
- Backup Port is a backup port that is ready to become the Root Port if the current Root Port fails.
- Rapid PVST+ ensures redundancy by maintaining alternate and backup paths in the network topology.

### Flash Card # 696

**BPDU Guard:**

- BPDU Guard is a feature in Rapid PVST+ that protects the network from rogue switches or unauthorized devices.
- When enabled on a port, BPDU Guard shuts down the port if it receives any BPDUs, indicating the presence of another switch.
- BPDU Guard helps prevent loops and ensures network stability.

### Flash Card # 697

**Root Guard:**

- Root Guard is a feature in Rapid PVST+ used to enforce the root bridge placement in the network.
- When enabled on a port, Root Guard prevents the port from becoming a root port if it receives superior BPDUs from another switch.
- Root Guard helps maintain the integrity of the spanning tree topology by protecting against unauthorized root bridge placement.

 

## Flash Card # 698

**Loop Guard:**

- Loop Guard is a feature in Rapid PVST+ that prevents the occurrence of spanning tree loops caused by inconsistent port states.
- When enabled on a port, Loop Guard monitors the consistency of received BPDUs.
- If BPDUs are not received on a designated port for a specified duration, Loop Guard places the port into a loop-inconsistent state, preventing forwarding.

## Flash Card # 699

**UplinkFast and BackboneFast:**

- UplinkFast and BackboneFast are optional features in Rapid PVST+ used to enhance network convergence in the event of link failures.
- UplinkFast enables rapid convergence by pre-selecting alternate paths in the network.
- BackboneFast reduces convergence time by quickly re-calculating the spanning tree topology when the root bridge changes.

## Flash Card # 700

**Bridge Assurance:**

- Bridge Assurance is a feature in Rapid PVST+ that ensures the integrity of the spanning tree by verifying bidirectional connectivity on designated ports.
- When enabled on a port, Bridge Assurance verifies that BPDUs are received on the port in both directions.
- If bidirectional connectivity is not verified, the port is placed into an inconsistent state until connectivity is restored.

 

## Flash Card # 701

**Verification Commands:**

- **show spanning-tree vlan <vlan-id>:** Displays the Rapid PVST+ spanning tree information for a specific VLAN.
- **show spanning-tree summary:** Provides a summary of the Rapid PVST+ spanning tree instances configured on the switch.
- **show spanning-tree interface <interface>:** Displays the Rapid PVST+ spanning tree status and port roles for a specific interface.
- **show spanning-tree root:** Shows the Rapid PVST+ root bridge information for each VLAN.

## Flash Card # 702

**Root Port Definition:**

- The Root Port is the designated forwarding port on a non-root bridge that offers the lowest path cost to the Root Bridge.
- It provides the shortest path for traffic from the non-root bridge to reach the Root Bridge.
- Rapid PVST+ selects one Root Port per non-root bridge for each VLAN.

## Flash Card # 703

**Root Port Election:**

- Rapid PVST+ calculates the path cost from each non-root bridge to the Root Bridge.
- The port with the lowest path cost on each non-root bridge is elected as the Root Port.
- Root Ports ensure optimal forwarding paths in the spanning tree topology.

 

## Flash Card # 704

**Root Ports - Role and Function:**

- Root Ports are designated as forwarding ports in the spanning tree topology.
- They forward traffic towards the Root Bridge and serve as the primary path for outbound traffic from the non-root bridge.

## Flash Card # 705

**Root Port Path Selection:**

- Root Port selection is based on the lowest cumulative path cost to the Root Bridge.
- Path cost is calculated based on the sum of individual link costs from the non-root bridge to the Root Bridge.
- Rapid PVST+ selects the port with the lowest path cost as the Root Port for each VLAN.

## Flash Card # 706

**Root Port Recalculation:**

- Rapid PVST+ recalculates Root Ports dynamically in response to changes in the network topology.
- If the current Root Port becomes unavailable or a better path is discovered, Rapid PVST+ reselects the Root Port accordingly.
- Dynamic Root Port recalculation ensures optimal path selection and network resilience.

 

## Flash Card # 707

**Root Bridge Definition:**

- The Root Bridge is the central bridge in a spanning tree topology, acting as the focal point for all spanning tree calculations.
- It is the bridge with the lowest Bridge ID (combination of priority and MAC address) in the network.
- Rapid PVST+ elects one Root Bridge per VLAN based on the lowest Bridge ID.

## Flash Card # 708

**Primary Root Bridge:**

- The Primary Root Bridge is the elected Root Bridge with the lowest Bridge ID in each VLAN.
- It serves as the reference point for determining the spanning tree topology and forwarding paths within each VLAN.

## Flash Card # 709

**Secondary Root Bridge:**

- The Secondary Root Bridge is the standby Root Bridge with the next lowest Bridge ID in case the Primary Root Bridge fails.
- It remains in standby mode and takes over the role of the Root Bridge if the Primary Root Bridge becomes unavailable.

## Flash Card # 710

**Root Bridge Redundancy:**

- Rapid PVST+ supports redundancy by electing both a Primary and Secondary Root Bridge for each VLAN.

 

- The Secondary Root Bridge acts as a backup in case the Primary Root Bridge fails, ensuring network stability and resilience.
- Root Bridge redundancy enhances network availability and fault tolerance.

## Flash Card # 711

**Root Bridge Selection Criteria:**

- Rapid PVST+ selects the Root Bridge based on the lowest Bridge ID, which consists of the Bridge Priority and MAC address.
- The bridge with the lowest Bridge ID is elected as the Root Bridge for each VLAN.
- Bridge Priority can be manually configured to influence the Root Bridge selection process.

## Flash Card # 712

**Port States - Forwarding State:**

- Forwarding State is the operational state of a port in which it actively forwards data frames.
- Ports in this state are part of the active forwarding path and pass user data in the network.

## Flash Card # 713

**Port States - Blocking State:**

- Blocking State is the operational state of a port in which it listens to BPDUs and does not forward data frames.
- Ports in this state are designated as backup paths and do not actively participate in data forwarding.

 

## Flash Card # 714

**Port Transition Process:**

- Ports transition through different states in the spanning tree topology: blocking, listening, learning, and forwarding.
- During initial convergence or topology changes, ports go through the blocking, listening, and learning states before reaching the forwarding state.
- Rapid PVST+ minimizes the time spent in each state to expedite convergence and reduce network downtime.

## Flash Card # 715

**Forwarding and Blocking Decision:**

- Ports transition to the forwarding state when they are selected as the designated or root port, actively forwarding traffic in the network.
- Ports transition to the blocking state when they are redundant or non-essential paths, preventing loops by not forwarding traffic.
- Rapid PVST+ dynamically adjusts port states to maintain loop-free operation and optimal spanning tree topology.

## Flash Card # 716

**PortFast Definition:**

- PortFast is a Cisco feature that enables rapid transition of designated switch ports from blocking to forwarding state.
- It is used on access ports connecting to end devices to minimize network convergence time.

 

- PortFast bypasses the normal spanning tree listening and learning states, immediately placing the port into forwarding state upon link-up.

**Flash Card # 717**

**PortFast Usage and Benefits:**

- PortFast is typically used on access ports connecting to end devices such as computers, printers, or IP phones.
- It reduces the time required for the port to become operational, improving user experience and network responsiveness.
- PortFast should not be enabled on ports connecting to other switches or network devices to avoid potential loops.

**Flash Card # 718**

**PortFast Limitations:**

- PortFast should not be enabled on ports connecting to other switches or network devices, as it can lead to loops and network instability.
- Care should be taken when enabling PortFast to ensure it is only used on access ports connecting to end devices.
- PortFast is not suitable for trunk ports or ports participating in spanning tree protocol operations.

**Flash Card # 719**

**Configuring PortFast:**

- PortFast is enabled on individual switch ports using the **spanning-tree portfast** command.

 

- It can be globally enabled for all access ports using the **spanning-tree portfast default** command in interface range configuration mode.
- Proper verification and testing should be conducted after enabling PortFast to ensure correct operation and network stability.

**Flash Card # 720**
**Term:** Cisco Wireless Architectures
**Definition:**
The design and deployment of wireless networks using Cisco wireless technology. It determines how wireless access points (APs) connect to the wired network and manage wireless clients.
**Examples:**

- Centralized Architecture
- Distributed Architecture
- Cloud-based Architecture (Cisco Meraki)

**Flash Card # 721**
**Term:** Centralized Architecture (Cisco)
**Definition:**
A wireless architecture where APs are managed by a central Wireless LAN Controller (WLC).
**Pros:**

- Easier to manage and configure
- Offers features like roaming, security, and QoS centrally
- Scalable

**Cons:**

- Requires a WLC, adding cost and complexity
- Single point of failure (WLC)

 

## Flash Card # 722

**Term:** Distributed Architecture (Cisco)

**Definition:**

A wireless architecture where APs operate independently and don't rely on a WLC.

**Pros:**

- No single point of failure
- Lower cost (no WLC needed)

**Cons:**

- More difficult to manage and configure (individual AP setup)
- Limited features compared to centralized architecture

## Flash Card # 723

**Term:** Access Point (AP) Mode (Cisco)

**Definition:**

The operational mode of a Cisco AP, determining how it interacts with the network.

**Types:**

- **Lightweight Access Point (LAP):** Relies on a WLC for management and control (centralized architecture)
- **Autonomous Mode:** Acts as a standalone access point with its own configuration (distributed architecture)

## Flash Card # 724

**Term:** Lightweight Access Point (LAP)

**Definition:**

A Cisco AP mode that depends on a Wireless LAN Controller (WLC) for management tasks like security, roaming, and configuration.

**Benefits:**

- Easier to manage centrally

 

- Offers advanced features through the WLC

**Drawback:**

- Relies on the WLC for functionality

**Flash Card # 725**

**Term:** Autonomous Mode (Cisco AP)

**Definition:**

A Cisco AP mode where the AP operates independently, managing its own security, roaming, and configuration.

**Benefits:**

- No need for a WLC, lower cost
- Works well for small deployments

**Drawbacks:**

- More difficult to manage individually
- Limited features compared to a LAP

**Flash Card # 726**

**Term:** Cloud-based Architecture (Cisco Meraki)

**Definition:**

A wireless architecture where APs are managed centrally through a cloud platform. (Think Cisco Meraki)

**Pros:**

- Simple setup and management through the cloud
- Scalable for large deployments
- Automatic updates and configuration

**Cons:**

- Requires internet connectivity for management
- Limited customization compared to on-premise solutions
- Potential security concerns with cloud storage

 

## Flash Card # 727

**Term:** Split-MAC Architecture (Cisco)

**Definition:**

An alternative to the LAP/WLC model where management and data forwarding are separated. (Not as common anymore)

**Details:**

- Combines features of centralized and distributed architectures.
- Uses a lightweight access point protocol (LWAPP) for communication.

**Note:** Split-MAC architecture is less common in newer Cisco deployments. It's important to be aware of it for CCNA exams but may not be a highly focused topic.

## Flash Card # 728

**Term:** Roaming (Wireless)

**Definition:**

The ability of a wireless client to seamlessly switch between access points while maintaining a network connection.

**Importance:**

- Ensures uninterrupted connectivity for mobile users
- Especially critical for applications like voice over IP (VoIP)

## Flash Card # 729

**Term:** Security (Wireless)

**Definition:**

Protecting a wireless network from unauthorized access and data breaches.

Common Methods in Cisco Wireless:

- WPA/WPA2 encryption
- Access Control Lists (ACLs)
- 802.1X authentication

 

Describe physical infrastructure connections of WLAN components (AP, WLC, access/trunk ports, and LAG)

**Flash Card # 730**
**Term:** Wireless Local Area Network (WLAN) Component Connections
**Definition:**
The physical cables and switch ports used to connect access points (APs), wireless LAN controllers (WLCs), and other devices in a wireless network.
**Components:**

- Access Points (APs)
- Wireless LAN Controllers (WLCs) (Centralized Architecture only)
- Network Switches
- Cables

**Flash Card # 731**
**Term:** Access Point (AP) Connection
**Definition:**
An AP connects to a network switch using an Ethernet cable.
**Port Types:**

- **Access Port:** Used for autonomous APs. The switch port carries traffic for a single VLAN (untagged).
- **Trunk Port:** Used for APs managed by a WLC (centralized architecture). The switch port carries traffic for multiple VLANs (tagged).

 

**Flash Card # 732**
**Term:** Wireless LAN Controller (WLC) Connections
**Definition:**
A WLC has several ports for different functions:

- **Distribution Ports:** Connect to network switches carrying traffic to/from APs (uses trunk ports).
- **Service Port:** Used for management and configuration of the WLC (access port).
- **Redundancy Port (Optional):** Connects to another WLC for high availability (redundancy).
- **Console Port:** For direct configuration and troubleshooting (out-of-band management).

**Flash Card # 733**
**Term:** Link Aggregation Group (LAG)
**Definition:**
A group of multiple switch ports bundled together to act as a single high-bandwidth connection.
**Benefits:**

- Increases bandwidth between the WLC and switch.
- Provides redundancy in case one physical port fails.

**Note:** LAG configuration might require specific settings on both the switch and WLC.

**Flash Card # 734**
**Term:** CAPWAP (Control And Provisioning of Wireless Access Points)
**Definition:**
The protocol used for communication between a WLC and Lightweight Access Points (LAPs) in a centralized architecture.
**Details:**

 

- CAPWAP runs over the tunnel created on the trunk port connection.
- It carries control traffic, data traffic, and management information.

**Flash Card # 735**
**Term:** VLAN (Virtual Local Area Network)
**Definition:**
A logical grouping of devices on a network that can communicate with each other, even if they are physically connected to different switches.
**Importance in WLAN:**
- Used to separate traffic for different purposes (e.g., guest Wi-Fi, corporate network).
- Tagged on trunk ports to differentiate traffic for APs.

**Flash Card # 736**
**Term:** Management Interface
**Definition:**
A dedicated network interface on an AP or WLC used for configuration and administrative access.
**Connection:**
- Typically connects to an access port on a switch for a dedicated management VLAN.

**Flash Card # 737**
**Term:** Power over Ethernet (PoE)
**Definition:**
A technology that allows delivering electrical power to an AP through the same Ethernet cable used for data transmission.

 

**Benefits:**

- Eliminates the need for separate power outlets for APs.
- Simplifies deployment and maintenance.

**Note:** Not all switches and APs support PoE.

## Flash Card # 738

**Term:** Antenna Types (Wireless Access Points)

**Definition:**

The type of antenna on an AP affects the range and coverage area of the wireless signal.

**Common Types:**

- **Omnidirectional:** Radiates signal in all directions (good for general coverage)
- **Directional:** Focuses signal in a specific direction (better for long-range)

## Flash Card # 739

**Term:** Site Survey (Wireless)

**Definition:**

The process of evaluating the wireless environment before deploying an access point network.

**Purpose:**

- Identify potential coverage gaps or interference sources.
- Optimize AP placement and configuration for optimal performance.

 

**Flash Card # 740**
**Term:** Mesh Networking (Wireless)
**Definition:**
A wireless network topology where APs connect to each other wirelessly, extending the network coverage.
**Benefits:**

- Useful for areas with difficult cable access (warehouses, outdoor spaces)
- Can provide self-healing capabilities if one AP fails

**Drawbacks:**

- Lower overall bandwidth compared to wired connections
- Increased latency due to additional hops

**Flash Card # 741**
**Term:** Wireless Standards (IEEE 802.11)
**Definition:**
A set of standards defining the protocols and specifications for wireless communication. (e.g., 802.11ac, Wi-Fi 6)
**Importance:**

- Determines factors like speed, range, and security capabilities of a wireless network.
- Compatibility between devices and access points.

**Flash Card # 742**
**Term:** Radio Frequency (RF) Spectrum
**Definition:**
The range of electromagnetic frequencies used for wireless communication. (e.g., 2.4 GHz, 5 GHz)
**Considerations:**

 

- Different frequencies offer varying range, penetration, and interference characteristics.
- Regulations may limit the use of certain frequencies in specific regions.

**Flash Card # 743**
**Term:** Power Levels (Wireless Access Points)
**Definition:**
The strength of the wireless signal transmitted by an access point.
**Configurable Settings:**
- Adjusting power levels can optimize coverage and minimize interference.
- Regulatory limitations may apply to transmit power in some areas.

**Flash Card # 744**
**Term:** Guest Network (Wireless)
**Definition:**
A separate Wi-Fi network dedicated for guest users, providing internet access with restricted permissions.
**Benefits:**
- Isolates guest traffic from the main corporate network for security reasons.
- Offers limited access for visitors without compromising internal resources.

Describe AP and WLC management access connections (Telnet, SSH, HTTP, HTTPS, console, and TACACS+/RADIUS)

 

### Flash Card # 745

**Term:** AP and WLC Management Access Connections

**Definition:**

The different methods used to connect to and manage access points (APs) and wireless LAN controllers (WLCs) for configuration and troubleshooting.

**Common Methods:**

- Telnet
- SSH
- HTTP
- HTTPS
- Console Port
- TACACS+/RADIUS

### Flash Card # 746

**Term:** Telnet

**Definition:**

A protocol for remote login to network devices. It transmits data in plain text, making it insecure.

**Use Case:**

Limited use in modern networks due to security concerns. Might be encountered in older configurations.

**Security Risk:**

Anyone can intercept the data transmitted during a Telnet session, including usernames and passwords.

### Flash Card # 747

**Term:** SSH (Secure Shell)

**Definition:**

A secure alternative to Telnet that encrypts data transmission during remote login sessions.

 

**Recommended Practice:**
Use SSH for secure management access to APs and WLCs.
**Security Benefit:**
Encryption protects usernames, passwords, and configuration commands from unauthorized access.

## Flash Card # 748

**Term:** HTTP (Hypertext Transfer Protocol)
**Definition:**
The protocol used for accessing web pages. In some WLCs (disabled by default), HTTP allows basic configuration through a web interface.
**Security Risk:**
Similar to Telnet, HTTP transmits data unencrypted. Not recommended for management access.

## Flash Card # 749

**Term:** HTTPS (Hypertext Transfer Protocol Secure)
**Definition:**
A secure version of HTTP that encrypts data transmission. Used for accessing the web interface of WLCs for configuration.
**Recommended Practice:**
Use HTTPS for secure access to the WLC web interface.
**Security Benefit:**
Encryption protects configuration data and login credentials during web management sessions.

 

**Flash Card # 750**

**Term:** Console Port

**Definition:**

A physical serial port on the AP or WLC for direct configuration using a terminal program and a console cable.

**Use Case:**

Useful for initial setup, troubleshooting, or recovery when remote access is unavailable.

**Flash Card # 751**

**Term:** TACACS+ (Terminal Access Controller Access Control System Plus) & RADIUS (Remote Authentication Dial-In User Service)

**Definition:**

Authentication protocols used for centralized user access control and authorization for network devices like APs and WLCs.

**Function:**

TACACS+/RADIUS communicate with a central server to verify user credentials and access permissions for management tasks.

**Benefits:**

- Enhanced security by centralizing user management.
- Auditing and logging of access attempts.

**Flash Card # 752**

**Term:** Default Credentials (APs & WLCs)

**Definition:**

Manufacturer-defined usernames and passwords used to access APs and WLCs for initial configuration.

**Security Risk:**

Leaving default credentials unchanged creates a security vulnerability. Anyone with access to the network can potentially exploit them.

 

**Best Practice:**
Change default credentials immediately after initial setup to a strong, unique password for each device.

## Flash Card # 753

**Term:** Management VLAN
**Definition:**
A dedicated VLAN used for isolating management traffic for APs, WLCs, and other network management devices.
**Benefits:**

- Improves security by separating sensitive management traffic from regular data flow.
- Prevents unauthorized access to management interfaces.

## Flash Card # 754

**Term:** Two-Factor Authentication (2FA)
**Definition:**
An additional layer of security requiring two verification factors for user login, beyond just a username and password.
**Examples:**

- One-time code generated by an app on your phone.
- Security token or fingerprint scan.

**Benefits:**

- Adds a significant layer of protection against unauthorized access attempts.

Interpret the wireless LAN GUI configuration for client connectivity, such as WLAN creation, security settings, QoS profiles, and advanced settings

 

**Flash Card # 755**

**Term:** WLAN (Wireless Local Area Network) Creation

**Definition:**

The process of configuring a virtual network within a wireless controller or access point to which clients can connect.

**GUI Settings (Typical):**

- SSID (Service Set Identifier): The name of the wireless network displayed to clients.
- Radio Band Selection (2.4 GHz or 5 GHz): Choose the appropriate frequency for your needs.
- Security Mode (e.g., WPA2): Encryption method to secure client communication.
- Pre-Shared Key (PSK) (if applicable): Shared password for clients to connect to the WLAN.

**Importance:**

Defines the basic parameters for clients to discover and connect to the wireless network.

**Flash Card # 756**

**Term:** Security Settings (WLAN)

**Definition:**

Configuration options to secure wireless communication and prevent unauthorized access.

**GUI Settings (Typical):**

- **Authentication Mode (Open, WPA2-PSK, WPA2 Enterprise):** Defines user access method (open or with credentials).
- **Encryption Type (e.g., AES):** Encryption algorithm used to protect data traffic.
- **RADIUS Server Configuration (if applicable):** Settings for an external authentication server (WPA2 Enterprise).
- **MAC Address Filtering (Optional):** Restrict access to specific client devices by their MAC address.

 

**Importance:**
Crucial for protecting your wireless network from unauthorized access and data breaches.

## Flash Card # 757

**Term:** Quality of Service (QoS) Profiles
**Definition:**
Configuration options to prioritize traffic for specific applications on the wireless network.
**GUI Settings (Typical):**

- Application prioritization (e.g., Voice over IP, Video conferencing)
- Traffic shaping/bandwidth allocation: Allocate bandwidth based on application needs.
- DSCP (Differentiated Services Code Point) Marking: Prioritize traffic based on pre-defined markings.

**Importance:**
Ensures smooth operation of critical applications (voice, video) by managing network resources effectively.

## Flash Card # 758

**Term:** Advanced Settings (WLAN)
**Definition:**
Additional configuration options for specific purposes within a WLAN.
**Examples (May vary by device):**

- **Beacon Interval:** Defines how often an AP broadcasts its presence.
- **Transmit Power:** Adjust signal strength to optimize coverage and minimize interference.
- **Fast Roaming:** Enables seamless client handover between access points.

 

- **Guest Network Options:** Configure a separate WLAN with limited access for guest users.

**Importance:**

Fine-tune performance, security, and user experience based on specific network requirements.

## Flash Card # 759

**Term:** Interpreting the GUI

**Definition:**

Understanding the layout, options, and functionalities available within the wireless controller or access point's web interface.

**Tips:**

- Look for tooltips, help menus, or documentation provided within the GUI.
- Familiarize yourself with common WLAN configuration terms.
- Consider the specific needs of your network environment when making configuration choices.

**Importance:**

pen_spark

Effectively configuring your wireless network for optimal performance and security requires understanding the available options in the GUI.

## Flash Card # 760

**Term:** VLAN Tagging (WLAN)

**Definition:**

Assigning a VLAN ID to a WLAN in a managed network environment.

**Purpose:**

- Isolates traffic for different WLANs on the same physical network infrastructure.

 

- Improves security by separating user traffic based on department, guest access, etc.

**GUI Settings:**

- Typically found within the WLAN creation or editing options.
- Select the desired VLAN ID for the specific WLAN.

**Importance:**

Essential for network segmentation and maintaining traffic separation in multi-user environments.

## Flash Card # 761

**Term:** Client Isolation

**Definition:**

A security setting that restricts wireless clients from communicating directly with each other.

**GUI Settings:**

- May be found under advanced WLAN settings or security options.
- Enabling client isolation allows clients to connect to the internet but not directly to other devices on the same WLAN.

**Benefits:**

- Improves security by limiting lateral movement within the network.
- Useful for guest networks or environments where direct communication between clients is not desired.

## Flash Card # 762

**Term:** Wireless Access Schedule

**Definition:**

Creating a schedule to control when the WLAN is active and allows client connections.

**GUI Settings:**

 

- Some access points or controllers offer the ability to set specific timeframes for WLAN availability.

**Benefits:**

- Conserves power when the network is not in use.
- Enforces access policies for specific times (e.g., guest access during business hours).

## Flash Card # 763

**Term:** Mesh Network Configuration (if applicable)

**Definition:**

Specific settings for configuring a wireless mesh network with multiple access points.

**GUI Settings:**

- May involve options for mesh formation, backhaul selection, and self-healing features.

**Importance:**

- Ensures proper communication and functionality within a mesh network topology.

## Flash Card # 764

**Term:** Monitoring and Reporting Tools

**Definition:**

Features within the GUI that allow you to view network performance metrics and troubleshoot issues.

**Examples:**

- Client connection status
- Signal strength and coverage heatmaps
- Network traffic statistics

**Importance:**

pen_spark

 

Provides valuable insights into the health and performance of your wireless network.

 

# Section - 3: IP Connectivity

 

**Flash Card # 765**

Define IP address.

An IP address is a numerical label assigned to each device connected to a computer network that uses the Internet Protocol for communication.

**Flash Card # 766**

What is IPv4?

IPv4 (Internet Protocol version 4) is the fourth version of the Internet Protocol, which uses a 32-bit address scheme.

**Flash Card # 767**

Explain IPv6.

IPv6 (Internet Protocol version 6) is the most recent version of the Internet Protocol, using a 128-bit address scheme to overcome the limitations of IPv4.

**Flash Card # 768**

What is CIDR?

CIDR (Classless Inter-Domain Routing) is a method used to allocate IP addresses and IP routing, allowing for more flexible allocation of IP addresses than with the older class-based system.

 

**Flash Card # 769**
What does DHCP stand for?
Dynamic Host Configuration Protocol.

**Flash Card # 770**
Describe DHCP.
DHCP is a network protocol used to assign IP addresses automatically to devices connected to a network.

**Flash Card # 771**
What is a subnet mask?
A subnet mask is a 32-bit number used in conjunction with an IP address to identify the network and host portions of the address.

**Flash Card # 772**
Explain NAT.
NAT (Network Address Translation) is a process used in routers to modify network address information in packet headers while in transit, typically to allow multiple devices to share a single public IP address.

**Flash Card # 773**
Define ICMP.
ICMP (Internet Control Message Protocol) is a supporting protocol used by network devices to send error messages and operational information

 

indicating, for example, that a requested service is not available or that a host or router could not be reached.

**Flash Card # 774**

What is a default gateway?

A default gateway is a device, usually a router that connects a local network to other networks or the Internet and forwards packets destined for addresses outside of its own network segment.

**Flash Card # 775**

Explain ARP.

ARP (Address Resolution Protocol) is a protocol used to map IP addresses to MAC addresses on a local network.

**Flash Card # 776**

What is a routing table?

A routing table is a data table stored in a router or a networked computer that lists the routes to particular network destinations, and in some cases, metrics associated with those routes.

**Flash Card # 777**

What is a hop count?

Hop count refers to the number of routers or gateways through which data must pass between source and destination.

 

### Flash Card # 778

Define VLAN.

VLAN (Virtual Local Area Network) is a logical network that defines broadcast domains in a layer 2 network. It allows network administrators to segment networks logically, improving network efficiency and security.

### Flash Card # 779

What is a static IP address?

A static IP address is an IP address manually configured for a device, as opposed to one assigned dynamically by a DHCP server.

### Flash Card # 780

What is a dynamic IP address?

A dynamic IP address is an IP address automatically assigned to a device by a DHCP server from a defined range of IP addresses for a specified period.

### Flash Card # 781

Define DNS.

DNS (Domain Name System) is a hierarchical and decentralized naming system for computers, services, or other resources connected to the Internet or a private network. It translates domain names into IP addresses.

 

**Flash Card # 782**

Explain port forwarding.

Port forwarding is the process of redirecting traffic destined for a particular TCP or UDP port on one network device to another device, typically to bypass network address translation (NAT) or to provide access to services on a private network from the Internet.

**Flash Card # 783**

What is a VPN?

VPN (Virtual Private Network) is a secure and encrypted connection established over a public network, typically the Internet, to enable users to access private networks securely.

**Flash Card # 784**

Define subnetting.

Subnetting is the process of dividing a single large network into smaller, interconnected subnetworks, or subnets, to improve performance, security, and manageability.

**Flash Card # 785**

Explain network segmentation.

Network segmentation is the practice of dividing a computer network into smaller, isolated networks, or segments, to enhance security, performance, and manageability.

 

## Flash Card # 786

What is a loopback address?

A loopback address, often represented as 127.0.0.1, is a special IP address used to test network connectivity on a device. It allows a device to send and receive data to itself.

## Flash Card # 787

Define a private IP address.

A private IP address is an IP address that is not globally unique and is reserved for use within private networks, as defined in RFC 1918.

## Flash Card # 788

Explain port security.

Port security is a feature used to restrict access to network devices by filtering MAC addresses on switch ports.

## Flash Card # 789

What is the purpose of a MAC address?

A MAC address (Media Access Control address) is a unique identifier assigned to network interfaces for communications on the physical network segment.

 

**Flash Card # 790**

What is a subnet?

A subnet, or subnet work, is a logical subdivision of an IP network into smaller, interconnected networks.

**Flash Card # 791**

What is packet loss?

Packet loss occurs when one or more packets of data traveling across a computer network fail to reach their destination.

**Flash Card # 792**

Define latency.

Latency refers to the time delay between the transmission and receipt of data over a network.

 

# Section - 4: IP Service

**Flash Card # 793**
**Term:** IP Services
**Definition:** Services and functionalities built upon the Internet Protocol (IP) that enable communication and resource sharing on a network.

**Flash Card # 794**
**Term:** DNS (Domain Name System)
**Definition:** A service that translates human-readable domain names (e.g., [invalid URL removed]) into machine-readable IP addresses, vital for accessing websites.

**Flash Card # 795**
**Term:** DHCP (Dynamic Host Configuration Protocol)
**Definition:** A protocol that automatically assigns IP addresses, subnet masks, default gateways, and other network configuration settings to devices on a network.

**Flash Card # 796**
**Term:** SMTP (Simple Mail Transfer Protocol)
**Definition:** A protocol used for sending and receiving email messages over the internet.

 

**Flash Card # 797**

**Term:** POP3 (Post Office Protocol 3) & IMAP (Internet Message Access Protocol) **Definition:** Protocols used for retrieving emails from a mail server. POP3 downloads emails to a local device, while IMAP allows access and management of emails on the server itself.

**Flash Card # 798**

**Term:** FTP (File Transfer Protocol)

**Definition:** A protocol for transferring files between computers over a network.

**Flash Card # 799**

**Term:** HTTP (Hypertext Transfer Protocol) & HTTPS (Secure HTTP)

**Definition:** Protocols used for communication between web browsers and servers. HTTPS adds encryption for a secure connection.

**Flash Card # 800**

**Term:** VoIP (Voice over IP)

**Definition:** Technology that allows voice communication (calls) to be carried over a data network like the internet.

 

**Flash Card # 801**

**Term:** SSH (Secure Shell)

**Definition:** A secure protocol for remote login to network devices, replacing Telnet which transmits data unencrypted.

**Flash Card # 802**

**Term:** VPN (Virtual Private Network)

**Definition:** A technology that encrypts data traffic and creates a secure tunnel over a public network like the internet, often used for remote access to corporate networks.

**Flash Card # 803**

**Term:** DNS Resolution

**Definition:** The process of translating a domain name into its corresponding IP address using the DNS system.

**Flash Card # 804**

**Term:** DHCP Lease Time

**Definition:** The amount of time a DHCP server assigns an IP address to a device before it needs to renew the lease.

 

### Flash Card # 805

**Term:** SMTP Authentication (SMTP AUTH)

**Definition:** An authentication mechanism used to secure email sending by requiring username and password on the mail server.

### Flash Card # 806

**Term:** FTP Modes (Active & Passive)

**Definition:** Modes used for establishing a connection between an FTP client and server (Active: client initiates connection, Passive: server listens for connection).

### Flash Card # 807

**Term:** HTTP Methods (GET, POST, PUT, DELETE)

**Definition:** Methods used in HTTP requests to retrieve (GET), send (POST), update (PUT), or delete (DELETE) data from a web server.

### Flash Card # 808

**Term:** VoIP Codecs

**Definition:** Algorithms used for compressing and decompressing voice data for efficient transmission over an IP network.

 

## Flash Card # 809

**Term:** SSH Key-Based Authentication

**Definition:** A secure method for logging into remote devices using a public/private key pair instead of passwords.

## Flash Card # 810

**Term:** VPN Tunneling Protocols (PPTP, L2TP/IPsec, OpenVPN)

**Definition:** Protocols used to establish secure tunnels for VPN connections (PPTP - less secure, L2TP/IPsec & OpenVPN - more secure).

## Flash Card # 811

**Term:** DNS Record Types (A, MX, CNAME)

**Definition:** Different types of DNS records that map domain names to various resources (A - IP address, MX - mail server, CNAME - alias for another domain name).

## Flash Card # 812

**Term:** DNS Caching

**Definition:** The process of storing frequently accessed DNS resolutions on a local device or server to improve response times.

 

### Flash Card # 813

**Term:** DNSSEC (Domain Name System Security Extensions)

**Definition:** A set of extensions to the DNS protocol that adds security features to prevent DNS spoofing and manipulation.

### Flash Card # 814

**Term:** DHCP Reservations

**Definition:** Manually assigning a specific IP address to a particular device within a DHCP pool for consistent addressing.

### Flash Card # 815

**Term:** SMTP Relay Servers

**Definition:** Intermediate servers used to send emails on behalf of other devices, often used in organizational email setups.

### Flash Card # 816

**Term:** FTP Data Transfer Modes (Binary & ASCII)

**Definition:** Modes used for transferring data files (Binary - preserves all data, ASCII - removes non-printable characters).

 

**Flash Card # 817**

**Term:** HTTP Status Codes (200, 404, 500)

**Definition:** Three-digit codes returned by web servers in response to HTTP requests (200 - success, 404 - not found, 500 - internal server error).

**Flash Card # 818**

**Term:** VoIP Quality of Service (QoS)

**Definition:** Techniques to prioritize VoIP traffic on a network to ensure smooth voice communication (low latency, minimal jitter).

**Flash Card # 819**

**Term:** SSH Tunneling

**Definition:** Creating a secure tunnel over an SSH connection to access other services on a remote server.

**Flash Card # 820**

**Term:** VPN Split Tunneling

**Definition:** A VPN configuration where only specific traffic is routed through the VPN tunnel, while other traffic uses the local network connection.

**Flash Card # 821**

**Term:** DNSSEC Record Types (RRSIG, NSEC)

**Definition:** Specific record types used in DNSSEC for digital signatures (RRSIG) and verification of non-existence (NSEC).

**Flash Card # 822**

**Term:** DHCP Scopes

**Definition:** Defining a range of IP addresses within a DHCP pool for specific purposes or network segments.

**Flash Card # 823**

**Term:** DNS Forwarders

**Definition:** DNS servers configured to forward unresolved DNS queries to another DNS server for resolution.

**Flash Card # 824**

**Term:** DHCP Lease Renewal

**Definition:** The process where a device requests to renew its IP address lease from the DHCP server before it expires.

**Flash Card # 825**

**Term:** SMTP Relay Restrictions

**Definition:** Limiting the ability of unauthorized devices to send emails through a mail server to prevent spam or abuse.

 

**Flash Card # 826**

**Term:** FTP Active Mode Firewall Considerations

**Definition:** Active FTP mode requires opening additional ports on a firewall to allow data connections from the server.

**Flash Card # 827**

**Term:** HTTP Request Headers

**Definition:** Lines of information sent by a web browser in an HTTP request that provide details about the request (e.g., user agent, requested resource).

**Flash Card # 828**

**Term:** VoIP Call Signaling Protocols (SIP, H.323)

**Definition:** Protocols used for establishing, managing, and terminating VoIP calls (SIP - simpler, H.323 - more complex features).

**Flash Card # 829**

**Term:** SSH Config File

**Definition:** A configuration file on a server that defines settings for SSH access, including allowed users, authentication methods, and port forwarding.

 

**Flash Card # 830**
**Term:** VPN Encryption Algorithms (AES, DES)
**Definition:** Encryption algorithms used to secure data traffic within a VPN tunnel (AES - considered stronger than DES).

**Flash Card # 831**
**Term:** DNS Record Time to Live (TTL)
**Definition:** The amount of time a DNS record can be cached by a resolver before it needs to be refreshed with the authoritative server.

**Flash Card # 832**
**Term:** DHCP Options
**Definition:** Additional configuration parameters that can be sent by a DHCP server to devices along with the IP address lease (e.g., default gateway, DNS server address).

**Flash Card # 833**
**Term:** DNS Dynamic Updates
**Definition:** Allowing devices to automatically register their IP addresses with the DNS server for dynamic hostname resolution.

**Flash Card # 834**
**Term:** DHCP Reservations vs. Exclusions
**Definition:** Reservations assign a specific IP, while Exclusions prevent a device from receiving any IP address from the DHCP pool.

 

**Flash Card # 835**

**Term:** SMTP Relay Authentication Methods (SMTP AUTH LOGIN, PLAIN)
**Definition:** Authentication methods used for SMTP relay, such as LOGIN or PLAIN, which require username and password credentials.

**Flash Card # 836**

**Term:** FTP Data Connections
**Definition:** Separate connections established for data transfer after the initial control connection in FTP.

 

# Section - 5: Security Fundamentals

 

**Flash Card # 837**

**Term:** Information Security (InfoSec)

**Definition:** The practice of protecting information assets from unauthorized access, use, disclosure, disruption, modification, or destruction.

**Flash Card # 838**

**Pillars:** Confidentiality, Integrity, Availability (CIA triad)

**Flash Card # 839**

**Term:** Threat

**Definition:** A potential cause of harm to an information system or the information it processes. (e.g., malware, hacking attempts)

**Flash Card # 840**

**Term:** Vulnerability

**Definition:** A weakness in a system, network, or process that can be exploited by a threat. (e.g., unpatched software, weak password)

**Flash Card # 841**

**Term:** Risk

**Definition:** The likelihood that a threat will exploit a vulnerability and cause harm. (combines threat and vulnerability)

 

**Flash Card # 842**
**Term:** Security Control
**Definition:** A countermeasure that reduces risk by addressing threats and vulnerabilities. (e.g., firewalls, encryption, access control)

**Flash Card # 843**
**Term:** Access Control
**Definition:** The process of regulating access to resources based on identity and permission levels. (e.g., user accounts, passwords, access control lists)

**Flash Card # 844**
**Term:** Authentication
**Definition:** The process of verifying a user's claimed identity. (e.g., username and password, multi-factor authentication)

**Flash Card # 845**
**Term:** Authorization
**Definition:** The process of granting permission to access a specific resource based on authentication. (e.g., user roles, access control lists)

**Flash Card # 846**
**Term:** Encryption
**Definition:** The process of transforming data into a scrambled format that can only be read by authorized users with a decryption key.

 

**Flash Card # 847**

**Term:** Security Patch

**Definition:** A software update that fixes a known vulnerability in a system or application. (important to keep systems up-to-date)

**Flash Card # 848**

**Term:** Social Engineering

**Definition:** The psychological manipulation of people to trick them into revealing confidential information or performing actions that compromise security. (e.g., phishing emails, phone scams)

**Flash Card # 849**

**Term:** Password Security

**Definition:** Creating strong passwords that are difficult to guess or crack. (use a mix of uppercase, lowercase, numbers, and symbols, avoid using personal information)

**Flash Card # 850**

**Term:** Firewalls

**Definition:** Network security devices that filter incoming and outgoing traffic based on defined rules. (can block malicious traffic)

**Flash Card # 851**

**Term:** Intrusion Detection/Prevention System (IDS/IPS)

**Definition:** Systems that monitor network traffic for suspicious activity and can trigger alerts or block attacks. (IDS detects, IPS detects and prevents)

 

## Flash Card # 852

**Term:** Backups and Disaster Recovery

**Definition:** Creating regular backups of data and having a plan to restore systems in case of a security incident or hardware failure. (ensures business continuity)

## Flash Card # 853

**Term:** Denial-of-Service (DoS) Attack

**Definition:** An attack that attempts to overwhelm a system or network with traffic, making it unavailable to legitimate users.

## Flash Card # 854

**Term:** Man-in-the-Middle (MitM) Attack

**Definition:** An attack where the attacker intercepts communication between two parties and can eavesdrop or modify the data. (e.g., on unsecured Wi-Fi)

## Flash Card # 855

**Term:** Phishing

**Definition:** A type of social engineering attack that uses emails, text messages, or fake websites to trick users into revealing sensitive information.

## Flash Card # 856

**Term:** Malware

**Definition:** Malicious software that can harm a system, such as viruses, worms, ransomware, spyware.

### Flash Card # 857
**Term:** Security Onion
**Definition:** A free and open-source Linux distribution pre-configured with security analysis tools for network security monitoring and incident response.

### Flash Card # 858
**Term:** Zero-Day Attack
**Definition:** An attack that exploits a vulnerability in software before a patch is available. (difficult to defend against)

### Flash Card # 859
**Term:** Penetration Testing (Pen Testing)
**Definition:** The authorized simulation of a cyberattack to identify vulnerabilities in a system or network. (helps improve security posture)

### Flash Card # 860
**Term:** Security Incident and Event Management (SIEM)
**Definition:** A system that collects and analyzes security events from various sources to detect and respond to potential threats.

 

## Flash Card # 861

**Term:** Multi-Factor Authentication (MFA)

**Definition:** An authentication method that requires two or more verification factors beyond just a username and password. (e.g., one-time code, fingerprint scan)

## Flash Card # 862

**Term:** Least Privilege Principle

**Definition:** The principle of granting users only the minimum level of access permissions necessary to perform their job duties. (reduces risk)

## Flash Card # 863

**Term:** Public Key Infrastructure (PKI)

**Definition:** A system that uses digital certificates and cryptography to verify the identity of users and secure communication.

## Flash Card # 864

**Term:** Secure Sockets Layer (SSL) / Transport Layer Security (TLS)

**Definition:** Protocols that encrypt communication between a web server and a web browser to protect sensitive data (like credit card information) during online transactions. (represented by a padlock in the browser)

 

**Flash Card # 865**
**Term:** Data Loss Prevention (DLP)
**Definition:** A security solution that helps prevent sensitive data from being accidentally or intentionally leaked or stolen.

**Flash Card # 866**
**Term:** Security Policies
**Definition:** Documented guidelines and procedures that define an organization's security posture and how employees should handle sensitive information and access systems.

**Flash Card # 867**
**Term:** Physical Security
**Definition:** Measures taken to protect physical assets, such as servers, data centers, and network devices from unauthorized access or damage. (e.g., access control systems, security cameras)

**Flash Card # 868**
**Term:** Security Hygiene
**Definition:** The ongoing practice of maintaining good security practices to protect systems and data. (e.g., patching systems, updating passwords, user awareness training)

 

**Flash Card # 869**

**Term:** Incident Response Plan

**Definition:** A documented plan that outlines the steps to be taken when a security incident occurs. (helps minimize damage and ensure a faster recovery)

**Flash Card # 870**

**Term:** Risk Management

**Definition:** The process of identifying, assessing, and prioritizing security risks, and then implementing controls to mitigate those risks.

**Flash Card # 871**

**Term:** API Security

**Definition:** The practice of protecting Application Programming Interfaces (APIs) from unauthorized access, data breaches, and other threats. (APIs are interfaces that allow applications to communicate with each other)

**Flash Card # 872**

**Term:** Cloud Security

**Definition:** The practices and technologies used to secure data, applications, and infrastructure in the cloud computing environment. (shared responsibility model between cloud provider and customer)

 

**Flash Card # 873**
**Term:** BYOD (Bring Your Own Device) Security
**Definition:** The security considerations and policies around allowing employees to use their personal devices for work purposes. (important to manage access and data security)

**Flash Card # 874**
**Term:** Security in Software Development Lifecycle (SDLC)
**Definition:** Integrating security practices throughout the entire software development process, from design to deployment. (helps build security into applications from the beginning)

**Flash Card # 875**
**Term:** Open-Source Security
**Definition:** The process of identifying and mitigating vulnerabilities in open-source software used in applications and systems. (requires careful evaluation and maintenance)

**Flash Card # 876**
**Term:** Social Engineering Techniques
**Definition:** Specific methods used in social engineering attacks, such as pretexting (creating a false scenario), phishing emails, and scare tactics. (Understanding these techniques helps identify suspicious attempts)

 

### Flash Card # 877

**Term:** Password Management Tools

**Definition:** Software applications that help users generate, store, and manage strong passwords securely. (reduces reliance on weak or reused passwords)

### Flash Card # 878

**Term:** Web Application Security

**Definition:** The process of protecting web applications from vulnerabilities that can be exploited by attackers. (includes input validation, secure coding practices)

### Flash Card # 879

**Term:** Insider Threat

**Definition:** A security threat posed by authorized users who intentionally or unintentionally misuse their access privileges. (important to have proper access controls and monitoring)

### Flash Card # 880

**Term:** Security Compliance

**Definition:** The process of adhering to industry standards and regulations related to data security and privacy. (e.g., HIPAA, PCI DSS)

 

### Flash Card # 881

**Term:** Threat Intelligence

**Definition:** The collection, analysis, and dissemination of information about potential security threats. (helps organizations prepare for and respond to attacks)

### Flash Card # 882

**Term:** Security Operations Center (SOC)

**Definition:** A central location where security professionals monitor and analyze security events, detect threats, and respond to incidents.

### Flash Card # 883

**Term:** Security Automation

**Definition:** Using tools and scripts to automate repetitive security tasks, improving efficiency and response times.

### Flash Card # 884

**Term:** Cyberwarfare

**Definition:** The use of digital attacks by nation-states to disrupt, disable, or destroy critical infrastructure and information systems of other countries.

 

**Flash Card # 885**

**Term:** Security Awareness Best Practices

**Definition:** Recommendations for users to improve their security posture, such as avoiding suspicious links, using strong passwords, and reporting phishing attempts. (Empowering users is crucial for overall security)

 

# Section - 6: Automation and Programmability

 

## Flash Card # 886

**Term:** Automation

**Definition:** The use of technology to automatically perform tasks that were previously done manually.

**Benefits:**

- Increased efficiency and productivity
- Reduced human error
- Improved scalability and consistency

## Flash Card # 887

**Term:** Programmability

**Definition:** The ability to create a set of instructions (program) that a computer or device can execute to perform specific tasks.

**Key Concepts:**

- Programming languages (e.g., Python, Java, Bash)
- Variables
- Conditional statements (if/else)
- Loops (for/while)

## Flash Card # 888

**Term:** Scripting

**Definition:** Writing a short program (script) to automate repetitive tasks.

**Scripting Languages:**

- Python
- Bash
- PowerShell

 

**Flash Card # 889**

**Term:** APIs (Application Programming Interfaces)

**Definition:** A set of instructions and standards that allows applications to communicate with each other.

**Benefits of APIs:**

- Enables automation between different tools and platforms.
- Simplifies development by providing pre-built functionality.

**Flash Card # 890**

**Term:** Network Automation

**Definition:** Automating network management tasks such as configuration, provisioning, and troubleshooting.

**Flash Card # 891**

**Configuration Management Tools**

**Definition:** Software tools used to manage the configuration of devices and systems in a consistent and automated way.

**Examples:**

- Ansible
- Puppet
- Chef

**Flash Card # 892**

**Infrastructure as Code (IaC)**

**Definition:** The practice of managing infrastructure (servers, networks) using code.

**Benefits of IaC:**

 

- Improves repeatability and consistency
- Enables version control and collaboration
- Simplifies deployment and configuration

## Flash Card # 893

**What are the main ways automation impacts network management?**

Automation streamlines repetitive tasks, reduces human error, speeds up configuration changes, improves network agility, and enhances overall network efficiency.

## Flash Card # 894

**Differentiate between traditional networks and controller-based networking.**

Traditional networks rely on manual configuration and management of individual network devices, leading to slower deployments and increased complexity. Controller-based networking, on the other hand, centralizes management through a controller that automates configuration and policies across the network, resulting in faster deployments, simplified management, and greater scalability.

## Flash Card # 895

**How does automation reduce human error in network management?**

Automation eliminates the need for manual configuration, reducing the likelihood of human errors such as misconfigurations, typos, and inconsistencies across devices.

 

## Flash Card # 896

**Explain how automation improves network agility.**

Automation enables rapid deployment of network services and configuration changes, allowing organizations to respond quickly to changing business needs and market demands.

## Flash Card # 897

**What role does consistency play in network automation?**

Automation ensures consistent configuration across all network devices, reducing configuration drift and minimizing the risk of network downtime due to misconfigurations.

## Flash Card #898

**Discuss the scalability benefits of automation in network management.**

Automation enables organizations to scale their network infrastructure more efficiently by automating repetitive tasks, reducing the need for manual intervention, and facilitating the deployment of new network services.

## Flash Card # 899

**What are some common automation tools used in network management?**

Examples include Ansible, Puppet, Chef, Python scripting, and SDN (Software-Defined Networking) controllers like Cisco ACI and VMware NSX.

 

## Flash Card # 900

**Explain the concept of intent-based networking (IBN) and its relationship to automation.**

Intent-based networking (IBN) abstracts network policies into high-level business objectives, allowing automation systems to translate these objectives into specific network configurations automatically, thus simplifying network management and operations.

## Flash Card # 901

**How does automation contribute to improved network security?**

Automation can enforce consistent security policies across the network, automatically detect and respond to security threats, and ensure compliance with regulatory requirements, enhancing overall network security posture.

## Flash Card # 902

**Discuss the impact of automation on network monitoring and troubleshooting.**

Automation enables proactive monitoring and troubleshooting by automating the collection and analysis of network data, identifying potential issues before they escalate, and automating remediation tasks to minimize downtime.

## Flash Card # 903

**Traditional Campus Device Management**

- **Definition:** Manual configuration and management of individual network devices (switches, routers) through a command-line interface (CLI) on each device.

 

- **Pros:** Granular control over configurations.
- **Cons:** Time-consuming, error-prone, difficult to scale for large networks.

## Flash Card # 904

**Cisco DNA Center Enabled Device Management**

- **Definition**: Centralized, software-driven approach using Cisco DNA Center to manage and configure network devices.
- **Pros:** Single pane of glass management, faster configuration, automation, improved security, easier troubleshooting.
- **Cons:** Requires Cisco DNA Center hardware/software investment, potential vendor lock-in.

## Flash Card # 905

**Automation**

- **Context:** Traditional vs. DNA Center Management
- **Definition:**
    - Traditional - Manual configuration for each device.
    - DNA Center - Automates tasks like configuration deployment, policy enforcement, and software updates.
- **Benefit:** Saves time, reduces errors, ensures consistency.

## Flash Card # 906

**Scalability**

- **Context:** Traditional vs. DNA Center Management
- **Definition:**

 

    - Traditional - Difficult to manage large networks with many devices.
    - DNA Center - Easily scales to manage a growing network with centralized control.
- **Benefit:** Simplifies network management for complex environments.

## Flash Card # 907

### Security

- **Context:** Traditional vs. DNA Center Management
- **Definition:**
    - Traditional - Requires manual configuration of security policies on each device.
    - DNA Center - Provides centralized security management, threat detection, and policy enforcement.
- **Benefit**: Improves network security posture and simplifies policy management.

## Flash Card # 908

### Troubleshooting

- **Context:** Traditional vs. DNA Center Management
- **Definition:**
    - Traditional - Requires manual investigation on each device.
    - DNA Center - Offers network health insights, simplifies troubleshooting with centralized visibility.
- **Benefit:** Faster identification and resolution of network issues.

 

## Flash Card # 909

**DevOps**

**Definition:** A culture and set of practices that combine development, operations, and security to deliver software faster and more reliably.

**Key DevOps Tools:**

- Version control systems (e.g., Git)
- Continuous integration/continuous delivery (CI/CD) pipelines
- Automation tools

## Flash Card # 910

**Robotic Process Automation (RPA)**

**Definition:** Technology that automates repetitive tasks typically performed by humans using a graphical user interface (GUI).

**Applications of RPA:**

- Data entry
- Customer service tasks
- Back-office processes

## Flash Card # 911

**Machine Learning (ML) for Automation**

**Definition:** Using machine learning algorithms to automate tasks that require decision-making or pattern recognition.

**Examples:**

- Network anomaly detection
- Security incident response
- Predictive maintenance

 

### Flash Card # 912

**Benefits of Automation in Networking**

- Reduces manual errors in configuration.
- Improves network consistency and compliance.
- Enables faster provisioning and deployment of new resources.
- Frees up IT staff to focus on more strategic tasks.

### Flash Card # 913

**Challenges of Automation in Networking**

- Requires initial investment in tools and training.
- Scripting and coding skills are needed.
- Debugging automated tasks can be complex.
- Security considerations need to be addressed.

### Flash Card # 914

**Idempotent Scripts**

**Definition:** Scripts that can be run multiple times without causing unintended changes.

**Importance of Idempotent Scripts:**

- Ensures configuration remains consistent after multiple runs.
- Reduces the risk of errors during automation.

### Flash Card # 915

**Version Control Systems (VCS) for Automation**

**Definition:** Software that allows you to track changes to code and scripts over time.

**Benefits of VCS:**

- Enables collaboration on automation scripts.
- Allows rollback to previous versions if needed.
- Provides a history of changes for auditing.

**Flash Card # 916**

**Testing Automation Scripts**

**Importance of Testing:**

- Verifies that scripts function as intended.
- Identifies potential errors before deployment.
- Helps ensure scripts are robust and reliable.

**Flash Card # 917**

**APIs for Network Automation**

- Examples: NETCONF, REST APIs, YANG models
- Allow programmatic access to network devices for configuration and data retrieval.
- Enable automation of tasks like switch port configuration, routing protocol settings, and device monitoring.

**Flash Card # 918**

**Continuous Integration/Continuous Delivery (CI/CD)**

- Automates the software development lifecycle stages of building, testing, and deploying applications.
- **CI:** Integrates code changes frequently and triggers automated builds and tests.
- **CD:** Automates the delivery of new code versions to production environments.

 

## Flash Card # 919

### Infrastructure as Code (IaC) Languages

- **Popular options:** Python (HashiCorp Configuration Language - HCL), YAML
- Define infrastructure resources and configurations in code files.
- Tools like Terraform and Ansible interpret the code to provision and manage infrastructure.

## Flash Card # 920

### Benefits of DevOps for Automation

- Faster software release cycles
- Improved collaboration between development and operations teams
- More reliable and consistent deployments
- Reduced risk of errors through automation

## Flash Card # 921

### Security Considerations in Automation

- Secure coding practices to prevent vulnerabilities in scripts.
- Least privilege principle for service accounts used in automation.
- Access control to limit who can run automation tools.
- Regular auditing and logging of automation activities.

## Flash Card # 922

### Robotic Process Automation (RPA) Tools

- Examples: UiPath, Blue Prism, Automation Anywhere
- Provide a visual interface to record and automate user actions on a computer.

 

- Useful for tasks with repetitive steps and clear user interface interactions.

## Flash Card # 923

### Machine Learning for Network Automation

- **Anomaly detection:** Identify unusual network traffic patterns that might indicate security threats.
- **Network performance prediction:** Proactively predict potential issues and optimize network resources.
- **Automated incident response:** Automate actions to mitigate network problems based on predefined rules.

## Flash Card # 924

### Benefits of Machine Learning in Automation

- Enables automation of complex tasks beyond human capabilities.
- Improves decision-making and problem-solving in network management.
- Allows automation to adapt to changing network conditions over time.

## Flash Card # 925

### Challenges of Machine Learning in Automation

- Requires large datasets for training machine learning models.
- Expertise needed to develop and maintain machine learning algorithms.
- Potential for bias in models based on training data.

 

## Flash Card # 926

**The Future of Automation and Programmability**

- Increasing adoption of AI and machine learning for more intelligent automation.
- Continued development of low-code/no-code automation tools for wider accessibility.
- Focus on automation that complements human expertise rather than replacing it.

## Flash Card # 927

**Debugging Automation Scripts**

- Common Techniques:
    - Print statements for tracing script execution flow.
    - Using a debugger to step through the code line by line.
    - Logging script actions and errors for review.

## Flash Card # 928

**Best Practices for Writing Automation Scripts**

- **Modular design:** Break down complex tasks into smaller, reusable functions.
- Use comments to explain the purpose of different code sections.
- **Error handling:** Implement mechanisms to gracefully handle unexpected situations.
- **Testing:** Thoroughly test scripts to ensure they work as intended in various scenarios.

 

## Flash Card # 929

### Infrastructure as Code (IaC) Deployment Tools

- Examples: Terraform, Ansible, Chef
- Interpret IaC code and provision infrastructure resources on cloud platforms or physical hardware.
- Automate tasks like creating virtual machines, configuring storage, and applying security policies.

## Flash Card # 930

### Benefits of Configuration Management Tools

- Reduce configuration drift and ensure consistency across devices.
- Simplify disaster recovery by easily replicating configurations.
- Enable rollbacks to previous configurations if needed.
- Improve collaboration and visibility into network configurations.

## Flash Card # 931

### Network Automation Frameworks

- Examples: OpenStack, Cisco ACI, Juniper Contrail
- Provide a platform and tools for automating network configuration, provisioning, and management.
- Often leverage APIs and programmable network devices.

## Flash Card # 932

### Benefits of Robotic Process Automation (RPA)

- Increased processing speed for repetitive tasks.
- Improved accuracy and reduced human error.
- Reduced costs associated with manual processes.

 

- Ability to work 24/7 without fatigue.

**Flash Card # 933**

**Challenges of Robotic Process Automation (RPA)**

- Difficulty automating tasks with complex decision-making.
- Limited ability to adapt to changes in user interfaces.
- Requires upfront investment in RPA tools and development.
- Potential job displacement concerns.

**Flash Card # 934**

**Artificial Intelligence (AI) for Network Automation**

- **Subset of Machine Learning:** Focuses on mimicking human intelligence for complex tasks.
- **Network traffic analysis:** Identify application types and optimize network resources.
- **Self-healing networks:** Automate network reconfiguration to resolve issues without human intervention.

**Flash Card # 935**

**Low-Code/No-Code Automation Tools**

- Provide a user-friendly interface for building automation workflows without extensive coding.
- Drag-and-drop functionality and pre-built components simplify automation development.
- Empower citizen developers (non-programmers) to automate tasks.

 

## Flash Card # 936

**The Role of Automation in Network Security**

- Automate security patch deployment across devices.
- Continuously monitor network activity for suspicious behavior.
- Automate threat detection and incident response procedures.
- Reduce manual workload for security teams.

## Flash Card # 937

**Infrastructure as Code Testing**

- **Unit testing:** Verify individual functions within IaC code work as expected.
- **Integration testing:** Ensure different IaC modules work together seamlessly.
- **Acceptance testing:** Validate that the deployed infrastructure meets business requirements.

## Flash Card # 938

**Infrastructure as Code Security**

- Secure coding practices to prevent vulnerabilities in IaC templates.
- Use of secrets management tools to securely store sensitive credentials referenced in IaC code.
- Role-based access control (RBAC) for managing access to IaC tools and resources.

 

## Flash Card # 939

### The Future of DevOps

- Increased focus on continuous improvement and automation throughout the software development lifecycle.
- Adoption of GitOps practices for managing infrastructure and applications using Git repositories.
- Collaboration between development, operations, and security teams will become even more crucial.

## Flash Card # 940

### Automation in Different IT Domains

- Automation is transforming various IT domains, including:
    - **Cloud computing:** Automating provisioning, scaling, and management of cloud resources.
    - **Security:** Automating security patching, vulnerability scanning, and incident response.
    - **IT service management:** Automating service desk tasks, provisioning user accounts, and resetting passwords.

## Flash Card # 941

### Ethical Considerations in Automation

- **Transparency:** People should understand how automation is being used and its potential impact.
- **Bias:** Automation algorithms should be developed and trained to avoid bias and discrimination.
- **Job displacement:** Strategies needed to support workers affected by automation through retraining and reskilling.

 

## Flash Card # 942

**Benefits of Automation in Cloud Computing**

- **Self-service provisioning:** Users can automatically provision cloud resources on demand.
- **Elastic scaling:** Automatically scale cloud resources up or down based on workload.
- **Cost optimization:** Automate processes to optimize cloud resource usage and costs.
- **Disaster recovery:** Automate disaster recovery workflows for faster recovery times.

## Flash Card # 943

**Automation Tools in Cloud Computing**

- Examples: AWS CloudFormation, Azure Resource Manager, Google Cloud Deployment Manager
- Define cloud infrastructure resources and configurations as code.
- Automate provisioning, management, and deletion of cloud resources.

## Flash Card # 944

**Automation in Security Information and Event Management (SIEM)**

- Automate log collection and analysis from various network devices and security tools.
- Generate alerts based on predefined security rules to identify potential threats.
- Automate incident response actions such as quarantining infected devices or blocking malicious traffic.

 

### Flash Card # 945

**Automation in IT Service Management (ITSM)**

- Automate service desk tasks such as ticketing, incident resolution, and change management.
- Self-service portals allow users to request services and track their progress automatically.
- Automate user provisioning, deprovisioning, and password resets.

### Flash Card # 946

**Automation Testing Frameworks**

- Examples: Selenium, Cypress, Robot Framework
- Automate web application testing to ensure functionality and identify regressions.
- Can be integrated with CI/CD pipelines for automated testing throughout the development lifecycle.

### Flash Card # 947

**Continuous Learning for Automation Professionals**

- Stay updated on new automation tools and technologies.
- Develop scripting and programming skills (Python, Bash, PowerShell).
- Learn about cloud platforms and APIs for automation.
- Understand best practices for secure and reliable automation.

 

## Flash Card # 948

**Citizen Developers and Automation**

- Employees outside of IT can leverage low-code/no-code tools to automate tasks in their roles.
- Enables process improvements and innovation without relying solely on IT resources.
- Requires proper training and governance to ensure responsible automation practices.

## Flash Card # 949

**The Future of Jobs and Automation**

- Automation will likely displace some jobs but also create new opportunities.
- Focus on human-centric skills like creativity, critical thinking, and problem-solving will be crucial.
- Reskilling and upskilling initiatives will be essential for adapting to the changing job market.

## Flash Card # 950

**Ethical Considerations in AI-powered Automation**

- **Explainability and transparency:** Understand how AI models reach decisions and avoid "black box" algorithms.
- **Fairness and bias:** Ensure AI models are trained on unbiased data to avoid discrimination.
- **Human oversight and accountability:** Maintain human control over critical decisions and hold AI systems accountable for their outcomes.

 

## Flash Card # 951

### Automation and the Future of IT

- Automation will continue to transform IT operations from reactive to proactive and preventative.
- IT professionals will focus more on strategic planning, automation governance, and managing complex IT ecosystems.
- Collaboration between humans and AI will be essential for maximizing the benefits of automation.

## Flash Card # 952

### Puppet

- **Declarative language:** Uses Puppet DSL (Domain Specific Language) to define the desired state of a system.
- **Agent-server architecture:** Relies on a central server (Puppet Master) and agents installed on managed devices.
- **Focuses on infrastructure as code**: Configurations are stored in code files, enabling version control and repeatability.
- **Widely used in large enterprises**: Popular for its security features and scalability.

## Flash Card # 953

### Chef

- **Domain-specific language (DSL) based on Ruby**: Uses Ruby syntax for configuration files (cookbooks).
- **Client-server architecture:** Similar to Puppet, with a central server (Chef Server) and clients (Chef Agent) on managed nodes.
- **Infrastructure as code and configuration management:** Offers a broader scope than Puppet, including application deployment.
- **Popular for DevOps:** Well-suited for automating infrastructure and application deployment processes.

 

## Flash Card # 954

**Ansible**

- **YAML-based language:** Uses YAML, a human-readable format, for configuration files (playbooks).
- **Agentless architecture (uses SSH):** No need to install agents on managed devices, leverages SSH for communication.
- **Simple and easy to learn**: Considered easier to learn than Puppet or Chef due to its YAML syntax.
- **Popular for network automation:** Widely used for automating network device configuration tasks.

## Flash Card # 955

**JSON (JavaScript Object Notation)**

- **Key-value pairs:** Data is structured using key-value pairs, similar to dictionaries in Python.
- **Ordered list of values (arrays):** Can represent lists of items in a specific order.
- **Nested objects:** Allows for complex data structures with objects containing other objects.
- **Lightweight and human-readable:** Easy for humans to understand and machines to parse.
- **Used for data interchange between applications**: A popular format for exchanging data between different applications and services.

## Flash Card # 956

**JSON Primitives**

- **String:** Represents textual data, enclosed in double quotes (").
    - Example: "This is a string"

 

- **Number:** Can represent integers or floating-point numbers.
    - Example: 123, 3.14159
- **Boolean:** Represents true or false values.
    - Example: true, false
- **Null:** Represents the absence of a value.
    - Example: null

## Flash Card # 957

### JSON Collections

- **Object:** An unordered collection of key-value pairs. Keys are strings, values can be any JSON data type.
    - Example: { "name": "John Doe", "age": 30 }
- **Array:** An ordered collection of values, enclosed in square brackets []. Values can be any JSON data type.
    - Example: ["apple", "banana", 10]

## Flash Card # 958

### JSON Syntax Rules

- Key-Value Separator: A colon : separates the key and value in an object.
- Commas: Separate key-value pairs in objects and elements in arrays.
- Whitespace: Spaces, tabs, and newlines are ignored for readability but not required.
- Quotes: All keys must be enclosed in double quotes. String values can also be enclosed in double quotes for clarity.

 

## Flash Card # 959

**Advanced JSON Features**

- **Escaping:** Certain characters within strings need to be escaped using a backslash (\) to be interpreted correctly.
  - Example: "This is a \"quoted\" string"
- **Comments:** JSON does not support comments natively. Use separate tools for adding comments to JSON data.

## Flash Card # 960

**REST-based APIs:**

- **Definition:** Representational State Transfer (REST) is an architectural style for designing networked applications. RESTful APIs allow clients to access and manipulate resources using standard HTTP methods.
- **CRUD Operations**: CRUD stands for Create, Read, Update, and Delete, which are the basic operations that can be performed on resources in a RESTful API.
- **HTTP Verbs**: RESTful APIs use HTTP methods, also known as HTTP verbs, to indicate the action to be performed on a resource. Common HTTP verbs include GET (retrieve), POST (create), PUT (update), PATCH (partially update), and DELETE (remove).
- **Data Encoding:** Data in RESTful APIs is typically encoded in formats like JSON (JavaScript Object Notation) or XML (eXtensible Markup Language) for exchanging structured data between clients and servers.

## Flash Card # 961

**CRUD Operations:**

- **Create:** Used to add new resources to the system.
- **Read:** Retrieves existing resources from the system.

 

- **Update:** Modifies existing resources in the system.
- **Delete:** Removes resources from the system.

## Flash Card # 962

**HTTP Verbs:**

- GET: Retrieves data from the server.
- POST: Submits data to the server to create a new resource.
- PUT: Updates an existing resource with new data.
- PATCH: Partially updates an existing resource with new data.
- DELETE: Removes a resource from the server.

## Flash Card # 963

**Data Encoding:**

- **JSON (JavaScript Object Notation):** A lightweight data-interchange format used for transmitting data between a server and a client. JSON is easy for humans to read and write, and for machines to parse and generate.
- **XML (eXtensible Markup Language):** Another markup language used for encoding documents in a format that is both human-readable and machine-readable. XML is commonly used for representing structured data in web services and APIs.

 

## About Our Products

Other products from IPSpecialist LTD regarding CSP technology are:

- AWS Certified Cloud Practitioner Study guide
- AWS Certified SysOps Admin - Associate Study guide
- AWS Certified Solution Architect - Associate Study guide
- AWS Certified Developer Associate Study guide
- AWS Certified Advanced Networking – Specialty Study guide
- AWS Certified Security – Specialty Study guide
- AWS Certified Big Data – Specialty Study guide
- Microsoft Certified: Azure Fundamentals
- Microsoft Certified: Azure Administrator
- Microsoft Certified: Azure Solution Architect

 

Microsoft Certified: Azure DevOps Engineer

Microsoft Certified: Azure Developer Associate

Microsoft Certified: Azure Security Engineer

Microsoft Certified: Azure Data Fundamentals

Microsoft Certified: Azure AI Fundamentals

Microsoft Certified: Azure Data Engineer Associate

Microsoft Certified: Azure Data Scientist

Microsoft Certified: Azure Network Engineer

Oracle Certified: Foundations Associate

Other Network & Security related products from IPSpecialist LTD are:

- Certified Cisco Network Associate Study Guide
- CCNA Routing & Switching Study Guide
- CCNA Security Second Edition Study Guide
- CCNA Service Provider Study Guide
- CCDA Study Guide

 

- CCDP Study Guide
- CCNP Route Study Guide
- CCNP Switch Study Guide
- CCNP Troubleshoot Study Guide
- CCNP Security SENSS Study Guide
- CCNP Security SIMOS Study Guide
- CCNP Security SITCS Study Guide
- CCNP Security SISAS Study Guide
- CompTIA Network+ Study Guide
- Certified Blockchain Expert (CBEv2) Study Guide
- Ethical Hacking Certification v12 Second Edition Study Guide
- Certified Blockchain Expert v2 Study Guide

www.ingramcontent.com/pod-product-compliance
Lightning Source LLC
LaVergne TN
LVHW081334050326
832903LV00024B/1152
*9798323357376*